THE Math with a Laugh SERIES

The Sticky Problem of Parallelogram Pancakes

& Other Skill-Building Math Activities

GRADES 4–5

Faye Nisonoff Ruopp & Paula Poundstone

HEINEMANN
Portsmouth, NH

Heinemann
A division of Reed Elsevier Inc.
361 Hanover Street
Portsmouth, NH 03801–3912
www.heinemann.com

Offices and agents throughout the world

Library of Congress Cataloging-in-Publication Data
Ruopp, Faye Nisonoff.
 The sticky problem of parallelogram pancakes : and other skill-building math activities, grades 4–5 / Faye Nisonoff Ruopp & Paula Poundstone.
  p. cm — (The math with a laugh series)
 Includes bibliographical references.
 ISBN 0-325-00926-0
 1. Mathematics—Study and teaching (Elementary)—Activity programs.
I. Poundstone, Paula. II. Title. III. Series.
QA135.6.R86 2006
327.7—dc22   2006006568

Editor: Leigh Peake
Production: Abigail M. Heim
Typesetter: Gina Poirier Design
Cover and interior design: Joni Doherty Design
Cover and interior illustrations: Michael Kline (www.dogfoose.com)
Manufacturing: Louise Richardson

Printed in the United States of America on acid-free paper
10 09 08 07 06 VP 1 2 3 4 5

To Charlie & Marcus,
for making my life infinitely joyful.

—*Faye*

To Toshia, Alley & Thomas E,
without whom nothing adds up. Thank you.

—*Paula*

Contents

Patterns, Relations & Algebra

Geometry

Measurement

Data Analysis, Statistics & Probability

Preface

When we first decided to collaborate on a mathematics book, we had in mind the creation of problems to be done during the summer. Schools have a long tradition of assigning summer reading; many teachers ask for parallel assignments in mathematics so that students do not lose ground over the summer months. Doing math in the summer—what a thought! Of course, many students will wonder why anyone would create math problems for vacation time. Believe it or not, we're sympathetic to that feeling. And that's why we've created a set of problems that we hope will be different from those found in standard textbooks—different in tone and style, but not in content. These problems are intentionally silly and humorous so students can laugh and be serious about the mathematics, all at the same time!

There has actually been some analysis of the benefits of humor in mathematics classrooms. In the December 2004/January 2005 edition of *Mathematics Teaching in the Middle School*, George and Janette Gadanidis and Alyssa Huang state,

> There are several benefits to using humor in the mathematics classroom (Cornett 1986, 2001; Dyer 1997; Martin and Baksh 1995; Medgyes 2002; Wischnewski 1986):
>
> • Humor helps create a more positive learning environment. It helps reduce barriers to communication and increase rapport between teacher and students.
>
> • Humor helps gain students' attention and keep their interest in a classroom activity.
>
> • By reducing stress and anxiety, humor helps improve comprehension and cognitive retention.
>
> • Humor improves students' attitudes toward the subject.
>
> • Humor helps communicate to students that it is okay for them to be creative; to take chances; to look at things in an offbeat way; and perhaps, even make mistakes in the process.

- Humor can help students see concepts in a new light and increase their understanding.

- The use of humor is rewarding for the teacher, knowing that students are listening with enjoyment. (10 [5]:245)

Although designed for use in the summer, these problems can also serve as a supplement to the curriculum during the academic year, as math to do at home with parents, as well as for skills reinforcement. Students need a change of pace and environment at times. These problems were created to provide entertaining contexts while keeping the mathematics content targeted and sound. The problems can be used as assessments, assignments, additional practice, or extra credit, as well as summer work. In addition, you will note as you scan the problems that there is a good deal of reading involved, making them an excellent tool for students to practice reading in context. We assume, then, that these materials could also be used for reading practice with students.

We ended up with a series of three books, one each for grades 4 and 5, 6 and 7, and 8 and 9. The content for these grade-level books is based on the focus areas identified in state and national standards. These areas, however, may vary from school to school. You may therefore choose to use problems from different grade-level books to accommodate your needs. Our goal was to make the materials as flexible as possible.

Whenever we look at mathematics materials, we tend to be curious about the authors, wanting to know who they are and why they wrote the materials at hand. So we've each included a short piece about ourselves, since we think our story is one that may both surprise and entertain you.

From Faye Nisonoff Ruopp

Paula Poundstone was a student of mine in the 1970s at Lincoln-Sudbury Regional High School in Sudbury, Massachusetts. Paula would say that she was never very good at math; I would say quite the contrary. I saw potential. Paula went on to be a highly successful comedian after she graduated, and we have remained close over the past thirty-two years. Paula now has her own children who are studying mathematics, and at times, I get calls (some of them late at night) about how to do some of the math problems they get in school. Once Paula told me that she made up stories for the problems to make them easier for her children to understand. Given her comedic talents, these stories turned out to be gems. And that's when the idea of collaborating on these books occurred to us. So now, after thirty-two years, she and I can proudly say that she has written a math book with her math teacher, an accomplishment that makes us both smile. We've come full circle, and we think this book is symbolic, in many ways, of the special relationships that students and teachers form, of the humanity that characterizes the study of mathematics, and of the belief that all students can learn and enjoy doing mathematics—and even smile through it all!

Many teachers hope to make mathematics playful and friendly for their students. I would like to extend the opportunity to parents as well. In thinking about my experiences as a parent doing mathematics together with my son, Marcus (who has far surpassed my mathematical abilities, I am proud to admit), I recall fondly the times when we sat down together to tackle a tough problem and the car rides when I posed problems such as "We've decided you can go to bed a half hour later each year. At some point you won't be going to sleep at all. How old will you be then?" He worked on that problem for an hour on our way to Vermont one weekend, not knowing anything about fractions. I also recall when he was about five, I asked him, "What would happen if you subtracted six from two?" His response: "You would get four in minus land!" His connection of mathematics to some fantasy world of negative numbers reminds me how important it is for children to experience their own inventions and perceptions of how mathematics makes sense to them. Likewise, Paula's fantasy contexts, rooted in humor and humanity, enable us to laugh while at the same time thinking hard about how the mathematics works.

From Paula Poundstone

How come math makes people cry? You'd think, of all subjects, history would be the tear jerker. But I cried over math when I was a kid. My mother used to cry when I asked her to help me. My high school math teacher and coauthor of this book, Faye Ruopp, kept a box of tissues on her desk, and if she ran out, class had to be canceled.

I can remember, when I was a kid, I'd get a word problem, something like: "Mary had four apples. She shared two of them with Joe. How many does she have left?"

Although I could calculate the remaining apples, I mostly wanted to know more about Mary and Joe and would often include that curiosity in my homework. Were they just friends? How did Mary get the apples? Why couldn't Joe take care of himself? What is it with Joe? Was that even his real name?

So when my own daughters were so frustrated and intimidated by their elementary school math assignments that they, too, followed the time-honored tradition of shedding buckets of tears over the wonderful world of math, I began to write personalized practice problems for them. Not surprisingly, once the problems seemed less serious, they relaxed a bit and much of the drama slipped away. We have also spent the last few summers doing a page or two of math each day and, no duh, both girls took a huge leap in their math ability as a result. I think the main thing is that it increased their confidence so they hit the ground running in the fall. We've saved lots of money on tissues and I'm hoping you will too.

I think the idea of our writing a book of these kinds of problems came from Ms. Ruopp. She had called me because she was going over her grade book from 1976 and noticed I still had some assignments missing. We got talking and I told her about doing math with my kids and the next thing you know...

And so we offer you these problems in the spirit of improving understanding and increasing rapport with your audience. We hope that when your students do these problems, they will smile and perhaps even laugh, and come to realize that mathematics can be fun and challenging and enlightening, all at once!

Acknowledgments

From Faye

My first memories of mathematics come from my paternal grandfather, Morris Nisonoff, who was a butcher in Jamesburg, New Jersey. He could add a column of numbers faster than anyone I know. I found that fascinating. My gratitude goes to him, then, for making calculations seem fun and accessible. To my own father, I express my love and gratitude for spending time doing math problems with me as a young child many mornings before I went to school. He thought a great way to start the day was to tackle two-digit multiplication! As an accountant, he too had a knack for working with numbers that transferred to both me and my sister, as we each eventually became mathematics teachers. My father, mother, and grandfather taught me the importance of doing mathematics at home with children, and the key role parents play in creating a positive disposition toward math. To that end, doing math with my own son, Marcus, has been a highlight of my parenting. I thank him, especially for continuing a tradition of math study as an applied mathematics major at Yale. His positive and joyful approach to mathematics mirrors his approach to life—how he makes me smile!

I would also like to acknowledge my past and present students, who taught me what it means to come to understand mathematics, and what it means to struggle with a subject that for many is formidable. Their spirit, humanity, diligence, and enthusiasm are continually inspiring. Teaching them has been a gift.

To my friends and family and colleagues in education who encouraged me to write this series, I thank you for your support and faith in this project. You will see yourselves in some of the problems we've created, and we hope they make you laugh.

I would like to thank Ellen Lubell for her impeccable legal expertise and advice in addressing the contractual issues, and for her support as a friend and confidante.

I extend my deepest gratitude to Leigh Peake at Heinemann, who had the vision and courage to support the initial idea for this project. I am indebted to her for her continued influence on the series. A special thanks to Michael Kline for his artistic genius in creating the cartoon illustrations, capturing the essence of the problems and adding to the spirit of the contexts. I also want to thank Abby Heim and Beth Tripp for their care, expertise, and mathematical acuity in editing the series.

And of course, my heartfelt thanks goes to my coauthor, Paula Poundstone, whose comic genius continues to inspire me. Beyond her creativity and sense of humor, she is a remarkable human being and a fabulous mother. Collaborating with Paula on this project has been infinitely rewarding—we laughed so much more than we thought we would! She has proven herself to be the mathematician I always knew she was.

And finally, I want to thank my husband, Charlie, for his unconditional support and calming influence throughout this project. As Paula's high school biology teacher, he also appreciated her amazing talent and encouraged our collaboration. This project never would have happened without him.

From Paula

The fact that I have been a part of the creation of a math book defies the laws of probability. Simple mathematical reasoning tells us that there must have been some other important factors that made this improbability possible.

I'd like to thank Leigh Peake at Heinemann for her kind support and skill. Someday I hope to remove a thorn from her paw.

I thank Abby M. Heim for making my part make sense.

I greatly appreciate the technical support of my assistant, Carmen Cannon, and that of my friend, Gordon McKee.

I will always be in the debt of my manager, Bonnie Burns, for clearing the path for me for thirteen years.

Faye Nisonoff Ruopp has been my friend, teacher, and mentor for thirty-three years. My admiration and appreciation of her grows exponentially each day. Without Faye, who knows what n would equal?

Number Sense & Operations

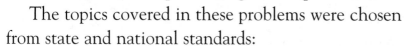

The problems that follow are in the Number Sense and Operations strand. The mathematics in these problems focuses on developing students' number sense as well as their computational skills. Students in grades 4 and 5 need to understand the meaning of operations, such as multiplication and division; they also need to acquire computational fluency, using efficient and accurate methods for performing these operations.

The topics covered in these problems were chosen from state and national standards:

- Understand place value to billions and thousandths
- Compare and order whole numbers, positive fractions, and decimals
- Perform operations (addition, subtraction, multiplication, division) on whole numbers
- Multiply decimals by whole numbers
- Multiply fractions by whole numbers

Multi-Digit Love

Much to the disappointment of the King and Queen, at the last minute, Cinderella called off the marriage with Prince Charming. "Come to think of it," she said, "I only danced with the guy that one night. What do I really know about him? Besides, he keeps singing." Eventually she left the kingdom and became a high school lacrosse coach and the Prince set out on another quest for a bride.

One bright morning, when the Prince had traveled far, far from his kingdom and strayed way off, deep into the woods, among the towering evergreens, the sweet scent of wildflowers, the clucking and scurrying of woodland animals, and the funny little birdsongs, just around the corner from the expensive coffee shop, he heard the thunder of countless feet. He looked up and saw marathon runners, as far as his eyes could see. Just as he tried to move out of their path, he tripped one and she fell into his arms. He apologized. She said, "No problem." Their eyes met and she jumped up and got back into the race.

The Prince was hooked. With a heart full of love, he ran from tree to tree singing of her beauty and about how his breath had stopped the whole time he'd held her. Most of the birds flew away. When he returned in despair to the castle and told his parents that, this time, he had found her, they said, "Where is she?"

"I lost her," he replied. They had so hoped he would outgrow this kind of talk.

"What did she look like?" they implored.

The Sticky Problem of Parallelogram Pancakes by Faye Nisonoff Ruopp and Paula Poundstone (Heinemann: Portsmouth, NH), © 2006.

"Heaven," said the Prince and he began to sing.

"Whoa, whoa, whoa, Mr. American Idol," said the Queen. "Did she have any identifying marks?"

"She was wearing a pinny," trilled the Prince. "It had a number 3 in the thousands place, a 5 in the ones place, a 7 in the millions place, a 0 in the ten-thousands place, a 2 in the hundred-thousands place, a 1 in the tens place, and a 6 in the hundreds place."

The Queen, not trained in math at all, took out a quill and paper and desperately wrote this note to you:

Dear Student,

Before the Prince drives the King and me crazy, please just tell me what the number on the runner's pinny was.

Your Friend,
The Queen

Help the Queen. Write the number.

The Sticky Problem of Parallelogram Pancakes by Faye Nisonoff Ruopp and Paula Poundstone (Heinemann: Portsmouth, NH), © 2006.

You're the Grand-Prize Winner

You are caller number 3,105,062,710 for the listener call-in contest on your favorite radio station, W-HAT! You win an all-expenses-paid camping trip with your favorite band. Soon you'll be walking up to the bathhouse to brush teeth with the lead singer while you make the drummer sweep out the tents. You'll be marshing marshmallows with the bass player and asking the keyboard player to stop playing a minute and fish the moth out of your hot chocolate. You can't wait! The only problem is that the radio host doesn't know how to say caller number 3,105,062,710 in words, which invalidates the contest and zips you right out of the tent. Write the number 3,105,062,710 in words for her or all you get is a W-HAT coffee mug.

The Sticky Problem of Parallelogram Pancakes by Faye Nisonoff Ruopp and Paula Poundstone (Heinemann: Portsmouth, NH), © 2006.

All Right, Everybody, Let's Line Up and Count Off!

If you made a good estimate of the population of the United States, would your estimate be in the thousands, millions, billions, or trillions? Remember to count yourself.

Same question as number 3, but for shoes on the side of the highway.

The Sticky Problem of Parallelogram Pancakes by Faye Nisonoff Ruopp and Paula Poundstone (Heinemann: Portsmouth, NH), © 2006.

Feeling a Fraction Happier About Fractions

Write the following fractions from least to greatest:

$$\frac{1}{8} \qquad \frac{1}{5} \qquad \frac{1}{2} \qquad \frac{1}{3} \qquad \frac{1}{50}$$

> HINT. Remember that the denominator (lower number) tells how many pieces the whole is divided into and the numerator (guess which) tells how many pieces of that size you have. For example, $\frac{1}{10}$ is one piece of a pizza that was divided into ten equal parts, and $\frac{1}{60}$ is one piece of a pizza that was divided into sixty equal parts. I'm a polite person. I say, "excuse me," to my cats. If someone offered me $\frac{1}{60}$ of a pizza, I'd say, "Thank you," and eat the sliver of pie, but deep down inside, if I was hungry, I'd rather have $\frac{1}{10}$. I don't want to tell you why. I want you to figure it out.

A. Fraction of a Fraction of Fraction Success
Find a fraction less than any in the previous list.

The Sticky Problem of Parallelogram Pancakes by Faye Nisonoff Ruopp and Paula Poundstone (Heinemann: Portsmouth, NH), © 2006.

Dick Digit's Number Depot

Leonardo Digit works at his dad's store, Dick Digit's Number Depot ("Where the whole family can shop for numbers and operations don't hurt a bit!") on the weekends. This weekend he asked his dad if he could please get off early to go with his friend Ed to a juggling class that Scoopy the Clown was teaching at the park. Leonardo could tell his dad was seriously evaluating the problem, because his mustache twitched as he distractedly put a shiny new box of fives onto a shelf.

"Leonardo, my delightful little product, naturally, like all parents, your mother and I want our children to know how to juggle, but last week's zero sale is over and the display window is still empty. If you can help me by putting the numbers in this box in the window in order from least to greatest, then of course you can go."

In the box Leonardo found a lovely set of the following numbers:

3.2   .32   3.02   30.02   .3002

He quickly and carefully displayed them in this order, for all the passersby to see.

.32   .3002   3.2   3.02   30.02

Did he go to juggling class? If not, please put the numbers in the right order so he can try again next week.

The Sticky Problem of Parallelogram Pancakes by Faye Nisonoff Ruopp and Paula Poundstone (Heinemann: Portsmouth, NH), © 2006.

The Biggest Whopper of a Problem Ever in the Whole World

The Exaggerators Club meets Wednesday afternoons in the small town of Rupertsville or "practically every day in the smallest town in the world," according to their poster in the library. Although the club includes some topflight exaggerators, their math skills are a bit limited.

The topic of their meeting this week was flips. Dizzy Flopman opened the meeting, declaring, "I once did 54 flips."

"Oh, yeah," said Bobby Bigman, "well, I did 5.4 flips."

"You guys are pathetic," boasted Tell-It-Tall Totter, flexing his arm muscle as he smoothed back his hair. "I did a mind-boggling, eye-popping $\frac{5}{4}$ flips."

Rosetta Donut practically jumped out of her chair to brag, "That's nothing: I did $\frac{4}{5}$ of a flip."

Wanda Whatnot announced, "I did 0 flips on Saturday 1,000 times. I'm exhausted."

"I'm available to coach you beginners anytime. I did .545 flips just last night," said Curly Hushup, puffing out his chest and adjusting his neck brace.

Susan Smugly sat with quiet confidence. Because she was the only one who hadn't yet spoken, all eyes slowly

The Sticky Problem of Parallelogram Pancakes by Faye Nisonoff Ruopp and Paula Poundstone (Heinemann: Portsmouth, NH), © 2006.

turned to her. Tell-It-Tall leveled his gaze on her. "How many flips can you do?" he challenged.

Susan beamed. " I can do $1\frac{1}{3}$!" she announced.

"Oh, man," the others chorused and slumped in their chairs with defeat.

These exaggerators could use a little help with their math. Could you put the number of the flips they claim to have done in order from least to greatest? And please don't use a calculator—the amount of practice you'll get that way is highly exaggerated.

Number Sense & Operations

The Math Problem That Could Save a Thousand Brussels Sprouts

When kids have math homework they sometimes ask their teacher, "Why do we have to do this?" in a whiny voice, with a look as though they're smelling over-cooked brussels sprouts.

Well, let me tell you something. The operations that you are about to perform without a calculator could come up in any number of dangerous situations that would make you thank your lucky stars that you practiced them here on this page.

A. Just as an example, what if someone who wasn't very nice at all and wasted water said to you, "You must add 345 + 1,247 correctly or eat an entire barrel full of brussels sprouts while running water in the sink with no drain plug"? I suggest you add those numbers.

B. Brussels sprouts are vegetables with a very distinctive taste. They're good for you and I want to encourage you to eat such healthy foods, but too much of anything can backfire on you (except math). What if, just if, you didn't get the correct answer to 7A and you found yourself choking down 1,247 brussels sprouts and, just as you chewed and swallowed the last one, you threw up 345 brussels sprouts and still felt gross, so you called the doctor and told him you had a belly full of brussels sprouts and you felt really disgusting? He'd say, "It's very important that I know exactly how many brussels sprouts are still in your stomach." Then what would you tell the doctor?

C. Do you see what I mean? I don't mean to frighten you, but there aren't a lot of people who like brussels sprouts. How do you think they get rid of them? These dangers exist.

What if someone who wasn't very nice at all and who often wasted water told you you had to multiply 29 × 123 or eat 29 plates of brussels sprouts with 123 sprouts each, while he hosed off the driveway? I suggest you do the multiplication.

D. I hate to even picture it, but what if you got an incorrect answer for 7C and as you finished up plate number 29 of brussels sprouts, you realized you actually liked them, and to celebrate, you invited 56 of your closest friends to a brussels sprouts hullabaloo, but your local produce store had only 1,792 of the little buggers? How many would each of your lucky guests get?

The Sticky Problem of Parallelogram Pancakes by Faye Nisonoff Ruopp and Paula Poundstone (Heinemann: Portsmouth, NH), © 2006.

Your Neighbor Is a Space Cadet

It has happened again. Your neighbor on the moon fell out of his moon rover while it was going. You've rushed to help figure out how far it's traveled. Quickly assessing the situation, you ask, "What speed was it set at?"

"It was going 30.2 miles per hour," he answers, still shaking the moondust from his boots. He points out the direction as you take a giant leap for mankind back to the spot he last saw the vehicle.

"And how long ago was that?" you continue while fishing a pencil from the bottom of your backpack.

"It was 2.9 hours ago."

Rats, your pencil point has broken off again and while you look for your sharpener, your paper falls up.

"Oh, for Pete's sake," you say, "I'll have to estimate. You'd better step back."

You fire up your jet pack and estimate the product of 30.2 and 2.9 to tell how many miles the rover has traveled. As you zip into space, you pass a strange, furry little creature in a helmet. You yell back down, "Your dog got out!"

So what did you come up with for an estimate?

Farmer Brown's Performing Pigs

Most farmers spend the year fattening up their pigs. Farmer Brown was up with the chickens each morning, helping his pigs stretch, toe tap, twirl, and sashay. They were much more than the other white meat to Farmer Brown. However, today's rehearsal wasn't going that well.

"Of the entire group of 12, two-thirds of you seem like you're not really serious about dancing in the interdenominational holiday pageant," Farmer Brown scolded his pigs. "And you know who you are." How many pigs with poor performing attitudes were a part of Farmer Brown's group?

If Pigs Could Fly Then We Wouldn't Have to Dress Them

"What's taking so long back there?" Farmer Brown boomed to an empty stage.

"We can't go any faster," came his wife's frazzled reply from behind the curtain. "It takes 24.3 seconds to get a sugar plum fairy costume on a pig and I've got 6 pigs to dress back here. Can't the goat stretch the Hanukkah song?"

How long would the goat have to extend her song for the 6 pigs to get dressed as sugar plum fairies?

The Sticky Problem of Parallelogram Pancakes by Faye Nisonoff Ruopp and Paula Poundstone (Heinemann: Portsmouth, NH), © 2006.

Extra! Extra!

Here are some extra problems so that these math ideas are safely secured in your brain, not teetering on the edge where they're likely to fall out if you think of anything but math for a minute. Nothing is sadder than spending a fun-filled day with friends only to realize that while you were laughing yourselves silly your number sense fell out of your head.

1. **What is the value of the digit 3 in the number 13,652?**

2. **Write the number 34,526,871 in words.**

3. Write the following fractions from least to greatest:

$$\frac{1}{3} \qquad \frac{1}{9} \qquad \frac{1}{20} \qquad \frac{1}{80} \qquad \frac{1}{5}$$

4. Put the following numbers in order from least to greatest:

5.26   52.6   .526   .56   5.06

The Sticky Problem of Parallelogram Pancakes by Faye Nisonoff Ruopp and Paula Poundstone (Heinemann: Portsmouth, NH), © 2006.

5. **Perform the following operations without a calculator:**

   A. 478 + 3,289

   B. 3,512 − 678

   C. 34 × 457

   D. 986 ÷ 34

   E. 35.7 × 8

   F. $\frac{3}{4}$ × 24

6. **Estimate the product:**

   39.8 × 5.2

The Sticky Problem of Parallelogram Pancakes by Faye Nisonoff Ruopp and Paula Poundstone (Heinemann: Portsmouth, NH), © 2006.

Teacher Notes

1. Multi-Digit Love

Problem 1 requires students to use their knowledge of place value. Students should know that in our number system, the value of each place is ten times the value of the place to its right. The order of the values to billions is ones, tens, hundreds, one thousands, ten thousands, hundred thousands, one millions, ten millions, hundred millions, one billions, ten billions, hundred billions.

In this problem, it is important to note that the order in which the numbers are given (3, 5, 7, etc.) by the Prince is not the order in which the numbers will appear in the answer. One approach is to begin with the smallest place value (the ones) and work forward to the largest place value (the millions). The answer is 7,203,615. Note also that a comma should separate each group of three digits, beginning from the right. Place value tends to be one of the content areas that is difficult for students, and time spent understanding this topic will prove useful in later grades as students work with decimals and operations with decimals.

2. You're the Grand-Prize Winner

Like problem 1, problem 2 focuses on students' knowledge of place value. In problem 2, students need to be able to write the number 3,105,062,710 in words. It may be helpful to think of periods, or groups of three numbers, when reading the number aloud or writing it down. The periods are ones, thousands, millions, billions, and so on. Whenever a comma appears, write the name of the period. The number the radio host must say is three billion, one hundred five million, sixty-two thousand, seven hundred ten. Writing the number in words forces students to slow down and clearly identify each place value by name and consider its order and value. Number names are also used in simple, everyday tasks like writing checks.

3. All Right Everybody, Let's Line Up and Count Off!

Problem 3 requires students to estimate the population of the United States. Interestingly, many students are not aware of population sizes, either local or global. For example, do they know the population of the town or city they live in or the state they live in? A reasonable estimate for the population of the United States is 300,000,000, and therefore the answer would be in the millions. This may be a good time to ask students to estimate the population of the world. (It is approximately 6.5 billion.)

Estimation of numbers—particularly very large and very small numbers—and judging the reasonableness of numbers is a core skill that runs throughout the grades.

The Sticky Problem of Parallelogram Pancakes by Faye Nisonoff Ruopp and Paula Poundstone (Heinemann: Portsmouth, NH), © 2006.

4. Feeling a Fraction Happier About Fractions

In problem 4, students are asked to order fractions from least to greatest. In this particular problem, each of the fractions has a numerator of one, which makes the ordering easier: The larger the denominator, the smaller the fraction (e.g., $\frac{1}{3}$ is smaller than $\frac{1}{2}$). If students are having difficulty understanding this, then you may want to use fraction circles or fraction pieces to illustrate the comparison by shading in the portion of the circle—or showing the fraction piece—that represents each fraction. Therefore we need only to look at the denominator in these unit fractions to order them: $\frac{1}{50}, \frac{1}{8}, \frac{1}{5}, \frac{1}{3}, \frac{1}{2}$.

Eventually students will learn to make comparisons among fractions whose numerators are numbers other than 1. But the more basic problem presented here is the foundation. In addition, in later grades students will order not only rational numbers but irrational numbers as well (such as the square root of 2).

Answers to problem 4A will vary. When looking for a fraction less than $\frac{1}{50}$, the least fraction in the list, we need to think about a fraction with a denominator greater than 50. For example, $\frac{1}{60}$ would be less than $\frac{1}{50}$. For an interesting thought experiment, ask, "What is the smallest fraction you can think of?"

This problem can be combined with problems 5 and 6 to create a series on the comparative values of factions and decimals.

5. Dick Digit's Number Depot

In problem 5, students are asked to order numbers with decimals. Some students believe, incorrectly, that the greater the number of digits,

the greater the number. That is, they might think .3002 is greater than .32 since there are four digits in .3002 and two digits in .32. In comparing decimals, it is essential to compare their place values. To do this, it is helpful to write the numbers one underneath another, so that the place values line up. Then, to compare the numbers, start at the left, since this is the greatest place value, and look for the first place where the numbers differ.

$$3.2$$
$$.32$$
$$3.02$$
$$30.02$$
$$.3002$$

In this case, there is only one number (30.2) that has a digit in the tens place, and therefore that number must be the greatest. There are two numbers (3.2 and 3.02) that have a digit in the ones place. The first place these numbers differ is in the tenths place. Since 2 is greater than 0, 3.2 is greater than 3.02. Therefore the correct ordering from least to greatest is .3002, .32, 3.02, 3.2, 30.02. It appears as though Leonardo did not go to juggling class. One way to extend this problem would be to ask for a decimal number that is between 3.02 and 3.03.

You can easily combine this problem with problems 4 and 6 to create a series on the comparative values of factions and decimals.

6. The Biggest Whopper of a Problem Ever in the Whole World

Problem 6 involves ordering both fractions and decimals. To compare these numbers, it is often helpful to put them in the same form. Students might choose to make them all fractions, but ordering them will still entail comparing fractions with unlike denominators. However, if all of the numbers are in decimal form, the comparison is much easier. Therefore, if we convert $\frac{5}{4}$ to a decimal, which is 1.25; $\frac{4}{5}$ to a decimal, which is .8; and $1\frac{1}{3}$ to a decimal, which is $1.\overline{3}$ to the nearest hundredth, the list becomes

$$54 \quad 5.4 \quad 1.25 \quad .8 \quad 0 \quad .545 \quad 1.\overline{3}$$

From least to greatest, using the technique described in problem 5, the number of flips is .545, .8, 0, 1.25, 1.33, 5.4, 54. In general, decimals are much easier to compare than fractions!

This problem can be easily combined with problems 4 and 5 to create a series on the comparative values of factions and decimals.

7. The Math Problem That Could Save a Thousand Brussels Sprouts

In problem 7 students are asked to perform the operations of addition, subtraction, multiplication, and division of two-, three-, and four-digit numbers *without a calculator*. These problems provide practice in whole number operations, skills that students in grades 4 and 5 should have mastered. If students are having difficulty with these problems, it is important to provide additional practice so that there is automaticity in finding solutions. By the time students are in the fifth grade, they should be familiar with standard algorithms for multiplication and division, or algorithms that are efficient, reliable, and accurate. Some may have learned alternative algorithms for multiplying (e.g., the lattice method or partial products) and alternative algorithms for dividing (e.g., the forgiving method, partial quotients, or the column method). These methods are useful because they underscore the importance of making sense of the operations and their underlying meaning, especially in relation to place value, before students encounter the standard algorithms.

For example, to compute the product 29 × 123 in part C, students could reason that

- 9 ones times 3 ones is 27
- 9 ones times 2 tens (or 20) is 180
- 9 ones times 1 hundred is 900
- 2 tens (from the 2 in 29) times 3 ones is 60
- 2 tens times 2 tens is 400
- 2 tens times 1 hundred is 2,000

They could then add these partial products to get the final answer:

$$27 + 180 + 900 + 60 + 400 + 2,000 = 3,567$$

If students are using the standard algorithms to do these problems, make sure they can explain their steps and reasoning.

The answers are

A. 1,592

B. 902

C. 3,567

D. 32

8. Your Neighbor Is a Space Cadet

In problem 8, students need to estimate the product of two decimal numbers. In this kind of problem, it is often helpful to round the decimals to the nearest whole number, or to numbers that are compatible so that they are easier to work with. (Compatible numbers make operations easier to perform; e.g., to estimate 99 ÷ 23, we might use 100 ÷ 25.) If we round 30.2 down to 30 and 2.9 up to 3, an estimate of the product would be 30 × 3, or 90 miles. Students should be encouraged to do these estimates mentally if possible. Students' estimation skills reinforce their number sense, and it is important to provide opportunities for estimation as often as possible. For example, on a car trip, students might estimate the time it will take to get to a destination or the distance between two cities in miles or kilometers.

9. Farmer Brown's Performing Pigs

There are several ways to think about multiplying the numbers indicated in problem 9. If students do not know the standard algorithm for multiplying fractions (the product of two fractions is the product of the numerators divided by the product of the denominators), it may be helpful to introduce an area model for thinking about the multiplication process. Area models are useful in that it is natural to think about the product of two numbers (length times width) when computing the area of a rectangle. Draw a rectangle with dimensions 1 by 12. Since we want the product $\frac{2}{3} \times 12$, we need to divide the side of length 1 into 3 equal parts, and then shade in the rectangle whose dimensions are $\frac{2}{3}$ by 12.

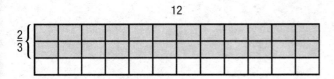

You group the small rectangles into groups of 1 ($\frac{1}{3} + \frac{1}{3} + \frac{1}{3}$). Counting up the number of small rectangles, each of whose area is $\frac{1}{3}$, we see that twenty-four of these small rectangles are shaded, and therefore the total area is eight. There are eight pigs with poor performing attitudes, then. Eventually students will be multiplying a fraction by a fraction, and this method of using areas of rectangles can also be applied to that situation.

10. If Pigs Could Fly Then We Wouldn't Have to Dress Them

This problem requires students to understand how to multiply decimals. If the standard algorithm for multiplying decimals has not been mastered, encourage students to use number sense

and estimation to guide their work. One way to think about this is to round 24.3 to the nearest whole number, 24, and then multiply: $24 \times 6 = 144$. Therefore we know the magnitude of the answer should be in the hundreds. Now we can multiply the numbers but disregard the decimals:

$$243 \times 6 = 1,458$$

Since we know from the estimate that the magnitude of the answer should be in the hundreds, we can deduce that the answer is 145.8.

Another way to think about multiplying decimals is to convert them to fractions. In this problem, convert 24.3 to $\frac{243}{10}$. Now multiply: $\frac{243}{10} \times \frac{6}{1} = \frac{1,458}{10} = 145.8$.

A foundation for this mental math is students' ability to multiply and divide with powers of ten. For example, what is $1,000 \times 10$? What is $10,000 \div 10$? Students have been known to use calculators to perform these operations, and they need to be convinced that doing mental calculations with powers of ten is faster!

Extra!, Extra!

1. 3,000
2. Thirty-four million, five hundred twenty-six thousand, eight hundred seventy-one.
3. $\frac{1}{80}$, $\frac{1}{20}$, $\frac{1}{9}$, $\frac{1}{5}$, $\frac{1}{3}$
4. .526, .56, 5.06. 5.26, 52.6
5. A. 3,767
   B. 2,834
   C. 15,538
   D. .29
   E. 285.6
   F. 18
6. 200

The Sticky Problem of Parallelogram Pancakes by Faye Nisonoff Ruopp and Paula Poundstone (Heinemann: Portsmouth, NH), © 2006.

$\mathcal{P}$atterns, Relations & Algebra

$\mathcal{T}$he problems that follow are in the Patterns, Relations, and Algebra strand. The mathematics in these problems focuses on developing fourth and fifth graders' ability to describe, generalize, and extend both numerical and geometric patterns. Students also analyze tables by describing rules that relate the inputs and outputs of functions. In addition, they begin to solve simple equations.

The topics covered in these problems were chosen from state and national standards:

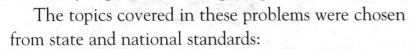

- Determine rules for extending patterns

- Analyze input-output tables

- Determine the values of unknowns in simple equations, for example, $43 - \square = 16$

The Pattern Problem

My daughter Toshia is a wonderful girl. She can be a bit difficult at homework time, though. When I asked her to please begin the pattern unit in her math book, she threw her pencil down, breaking the point, and yelled, "I hate patterns. I hate patterns. I hate patterns, and you can't make me do them. I hate patterns. I hate patterns. I hate patterns, and you can't make me do them. I hate patterns...."

I hid behind a big chair. What do you think she said next? Explain the pattern.

The Sticky Problem of Parallelogram Pancakes by Faye Nisonoff Ruopp and Paula Poundstone (Heinemann: Portsmouth, NH), © 2006.

The Dog Who Dog-Eared the Page

Late at night I often hear the suctionlike sound of my dog Cal's sticky, gloppy lips opening and the swishing sound of his long tongue dragging across what I thought was his dirty fur. But a few weeks ago I noticed my *Old Yeller* book laying on the floor near the dog's bed. As I picked it up to return it to the shelf, it fell open to page 3, where I noticed a paw print and a wee bit of dog spit. The next day I found the book off the shelf again and the paw print was on page 7. The following day I found it marked on page 11, and on page 15 the day after that.

My insane black lab, German shepherd, pit bull, and chow mutt wasn't bathing in the middle of the night; he was flipping the pages of *Old Yeller*. I know for sure because about a month later I heard him crying late at night and, sure enough, he was on the last page. I don't have to be Sherlock Holmes to figure that out, but what about the pattern? Can you determine a rule for finding the next page number he stopped on after page 15?

The Sticky Problem of Parallelogram Pancakes by Faye Nisonoff Ruopp and Paula Poundstone (Heinemann: Portsmouth, NH), © 2006.

Lizard Graffiti

My bearded dragon lizard, Daisy, scratches and bangs her lizard lips on the glass wall of her tank. I always assumed she wanted out, but one day she got out and I found her scratching and banging her lizard lips on the outside of the glass.

She's got to be pretty smart, that Daisy, because a few days ago, while I placed her lovingly prepared chopped salad into her tank, I saw that she had drawn this figure on the glass:

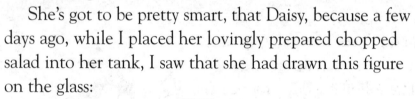

The next day she had drawn this figure:

When I looked again, it looked like this:

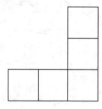

The Sticky Problem of Parallelogram Pancakes by Faye Nisonoff Ruopp and Paula Poundstone (Heinemann: Portsmouth, NH), © 2006.

Both Daisy and I have read *Charlotte's Web*, so we know animals can do remarkable things, but you always think these things happen to other people and not yourself, you know? What do you think the figure looked like the next time I looked? And the time after that?

The Sticky Problem of Parallelogram Pancakes by Faye Nisonoff Ruopp and Paula Poundstone (Heinemann: Portsmouth, NH), © 2006.

The Terrifying Tale of Flossing Fiends

Alley had long suspected her orthodontist's assistant was a little off. After all, what kind of job is that? Talking to kids with crooked teeth while their mouths are opened and they're practically upside down. And the kids can't even use consonants when they talk to her because her hands are in their mouths. Did the woman study that language in school? What is it, Vowelish? Alley thought the orthodontist's assistant must have studied Vowelish in orthodontist's assistant school because when she managed to blurt out, "Ayiouooaaoo," from behind the woman's hands, she responded, "Why, yes, Alley, you may use the restroom."

Alley scrambled down from the chair and headed toward the restroom, but she accidentally pushed open the wrong door. She found herself in a huge room, facing an enormous metal box with a slide at the top and a revolving door on its side. A loud rumbling noise accompanied by a clanging and clashing was coming from within the box. The lights dimmed. Something felt beyond the bounds of normal orthodontia. Fortunately, Alley had read a lot of scary books, so she knew that no one could possibly see her if she crouched quickly behind the door she had opened while she checked out this weird situation. She watched in awe (which means, "you dropped the purple rubber bands in my mouth," in Vowelish, but in

The Sticky Problem of Parallelogram Pancakes by Faye Nisonoff Ruopp and Paula Poundstone (Heinemann: Portsmouth, NH), © 2006.

English it means amazement). So Alley watch in awe as 2 identical orthodontist's assistants climbed up a ladder and slid down the slide into the machine. A few seconds later the revolving door spun around, releasing 7 orthodontist's assistants into the room, nodding and smiling and asking no one in particular, "And where do you go to school?" Faster than you can floss a tooth, 3 orthodontist's assistants zipped down the slide and 10 came out, wagging their fingers and saying, "Never put your retainer in a napkin." A second later, 4 orthodontist's assistants plunged into the machine and 13 came out, each with a sympathetic look on her face, saying, "You may feel some discomfort."

Alley didn't like to think about patterns, because they had always upset her older sister, Toshia, so much, but something odd was going on here. When 5 more orthodontist's assistants entered the machine and 16 came out, she knew she had to determine what was going on in that machine so she could tell the police—or at least the receptionist. What was the rule relating the inputs and the outputs of the terrifying machine? If you need a table, here it is:

INPUT	OUTPUT
2	7
3	10
4	13
5	16

The Sticky Problem of Parallelogram Pancakes by Faye Nisonoff Ruopp and Paula Poundstone (Heinemann: Portsmouth, NH), © 2006.

Two Heads Are Worse Than One

You've been living on the moon for a while now, and things are going well. Your Ping-Pong serve is fantastic up there. It was well worth the trip. The atmosphere is a little gray, but your colorful shower curtain has done wonders to brighten the place up.

However, something absolutely freaky happened the other day or night; it's tough to tell. You had just finished a yummy tube of pizza when you noticed a circular area of moondust on the ground that seemed to be glowing. There was nothing there at first—zero, nothing, empty. But the dust seemed to flicker and out popped a creepy, writhing, fat caterpillar with a face on both ends, singing both parts of a round of "Row, Row, Row Your Boat."

It was so gross. Maybe it wasn't the right thing to do, but you freaked out, assumed your karate stance, and with lightning speed, chopped the repulsive creature into 4 parts. Don't feel too bad; it didn't die. In fact, each of the parts grew heads and continued to sing. So, you buried the 4 creatures in the glowing ground.

"Phew," you thought, holding out your "Row, Row, Row Your Boat"-singing-two-headed-caterpillar-type-creature-gooed hands, so the goo wouldn't get on the sleeves of your space suit. The next thing you knew, you heard the song again, this time with more voices. You could not believe your eyes when you saw 9 disgusting,

The Sticky Problem of Parallelogram Pancakes by Faye Nisonoff Ruopp and Paula Poundstone (Heinemann: Portsmouth, NH), © 2006.

two-headed, puffy, fat caterpillar-type creatures crawling out from under the dirt, belting out a cacophony of "Row, Row, Row Your Boat" in an almost demanding tone, as though you actually should be row, rowing your boat ever so gently down a stream.

Quickly, you used your scientific brain to experiment. You separated 2 nauseating, two-headed, wriggling caterpillar-type creatures from the pack and buried them there in the glowing circular patch. You picked the ones that didn't seem to know the words. They just kept singing, "Row, row, row, row, row…" It was really wrecking the song. You buried them, just to see what would happen. Soon, 5 creatures sprung out of the ground, blaring a round of "Row, Row, Row Your Boat." Then, with your gooey hands over your ears, you scraped some glowing moondust over 6 of the worst singers, and seconds later 13 horrifying two-headed caterpillar-type whatever-the-heck-they-were crawled out, practically shouting for you to get your oars in the water and zip your boat gently down the stream. Now, if you can possibly hear me, I would like you to tell me, what on earth (or moon) is going on under that moodust? What's the rule for how many go in and how many come out?

HINT. Make a table showing how many two-headed caterpillar-type creatures went in and how many came out each time.

The Sticky Problem of Parallelogram Pancakes by Faye Nisonoff Ruopp and Paula Poundstone (Heinemann: Portsmouth, NH), © 2006.

The Greatest Rock and Roll Band That Ever Toasted a Wienie

You recently won a camping trip with your favorite rock band from radio station W-HAT. Until now, everything was going well.

Now, as you walked up the hill from the bath-house, where you scrubbed the burned oatmeal from the bottom of your camping cookware, you could hear your tentmates shouting. The "Dude"s and "Man"s were getting more furious as you approached.

"Dude!"

"Dude!"

"Aw, man!"

"Dude...Du-ude."

"Dude, I think the ceiling's supposed to be higher than two inches."

These guys were good musicians, one of them even had a goatee, but they were not so good with tent poles as it turned out. You couldn't tell from their CD cover.

You knew it was gonna be a long night if you couldn't figure out how many tent-pole segments were missing, so you did. There used to be 43 and now there were only 16. You told the drummer that solving the following equation would reveal the number that was missing. He said, "Dude." So find the value for □ in

$$43 - \square = 16$$

The Sticky Problem of Parallelogram Pancakes by Faye Nisonoff Ruopp and Paula Poundstone (Heinemann: Portsmouth, NH), © 2006.

The Bushy Tale of Sour Squirrels

The camping trip with your favorite rock band was starting to go sour. You could already tell by the pucker on their little lips as they ran from your food box that the squirrels had eaten most of the super-sour lemon cookies. The bass player yelled, "Dude!"

Only a bag of 15 was left untouched. Two of the band guys liked supersour lemon cookies, too, so you said, "I'll just take 3 and you 2 split the rest."

"Yeah, but how many do we each get?" pouted the drummer.

Of course, you told him that they needed to solve this equation:

$$2 \times \square + 3 = 15$$

"Dude."

The Sticky Problem of Parallelogram Pancakes by Faye Nisonoff Ruopp and Paula Poundstone (Heinemann: Portsmouth, NH), © 2006.

Extra! Extra!

I know you might be upset about these extra patterns, relations, and algebra questions, but after you do two you'll feel better, then you might get upset again, but after two more you'll feel better, then you might get upset again, but after two more you'll feel better, and then you might get upset again, but what do you think will happen when you do two more?

1. **Find a rule for determining the next number in the following pattern:**

    4   9   14   19 ...

2. **What might be the next two figures in this pattern?**

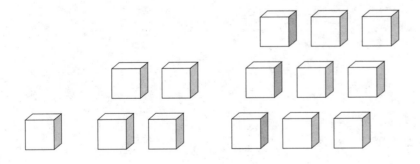

   The Sticky Problem of Parallelogram Pancakes by Faye Nisonoff Ruopp and Paula Poundstone (Heinemann: Portsmouth, NH), © 2006.

3. Find a rule for the following input-output table:

INPUT	OUTPUT
1	7
2	12
3	17
4	22

4. Find the value of the box in this equation:

$$3 \times \square - 4 = 11.$$

The Sticky Problem of Parallelogram Pancakes by Faye Nisonoff Ruopp and Paula Poundstone (Heinemann: Portsmouth, NH), © 2006.

Teacher Notes

1. The Pattern Problem

In problem 1, students need to think about the pattern in Toshia's responses. She repeats "I hate patterns" twice and then says, "I hate patterns, and you can't make me do them." The pattern, then, consists of these three sentences. Her next statement would be, "I hate patterns."

2. The Dog Who Dog-Eared the Page

Problem 2 focuses on a numerical pattern for which the students need to find the next term in a sequence. When given a numerical sequence, it is sometimes helpful to think about the four operations in arithmetic (addition, subtraction, multiplication, and division) and how they might apply when going from one term of the sequence to the next. The object is to find one rule that will work for every term of the sequence. The easiest operation to explore is addition, and many students will quickly observe that to get from 3 (the first term of the sequence, referring to the page number with the first paw print) to 7 (the second term of the sequence, referring to the page the second paw print was on), we must add 4; to get from 7 to 11, we must add 4 as well; and to get from 11 to 15, again we must add 4. Therefore one rule that works for all of the numbers of the sequence is: to get any term in the sequence, add four to the previous term. (This, by the way, is a recursive definition of a sequence, one that tells us how to get to the next term if we know the term before.)

Therefore, the next term in the sequence would be 19 (15 + 4 = 19). As a challenge, ask students what the one-hundredth term of the sequence would be; students will encounter this type of problem in later middle school grades.

3. Lizard Graffiti

In problem 3, students are given a visual pattern that they are asked to continue. For many students, using blocks or tiles to create the first three stages of the pattern is helpful. As students build the pattern, they often gain insights into the rule for the pattern. For example, think of a way to get from stage 2 of this pattern (the second figure drawn by Daisy) to stage 3, starting with the building of stage 2. We might think of adding two tiles or squares to the ends of the "legs" of the pattern. This would also be true when going from the first stage to the second—we add two squares to the single tile, which becomes the corner of the second stage. Thus, to get from the third stage to the fourth stage, we would again add two squares, one to each end, and repeat this for the next stage, to obtain the following:

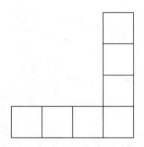

The Sticky Problem of Parallelogram Pancakes by Faye Nisonoff Ruopp and Paula Poundstone (Heinemann: Portsmouth, NH), © 2006.

Some students will see a different way to go from one stage to another. They might look at the third stage, for example, as one leg of three squares and one leg of two squares.

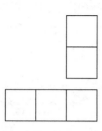

Likewise, they might see the second stage as a leg of two squares and a leg of one.

Therefore, the fourth stage would be a leg of four squares and a leg of three squares.

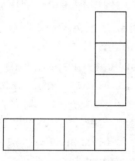

For those students who might enjoy a challenge, ask them to think about what the figure would like in the one-hundredth stage, or even better, at any stage. Their ability to predict these subsequent stages, in cases that are difficult to draw or write out, marks the transition from arithmetic to algebraic thinking, as students think of ways to generalize the process down the line.

4. The Terrifying Tale of Flossing Fiends

Problem 4 is very similar to problem 2 in the strategies that students might use to figure out a rule for getting from any input to its corresponding output in the table. Again, this rule must work for every input-output pair. One pattern that students often look for is any constant number that can be added to one output to get the next. For example, looking at the Output column of the table, to get from 7 to 10, we add 3. To get from 10 to 13, we add 3 again. To get from 13 to 16, we add 3 yet again. Therefore, it appears that there is a constant difference of 3 in the output column. This difference gives clues to the rule for the table if we think of repeatedly adding 3 as multiplication by 3. Often this is the first definition of multiplication that students are given in earlier grades: repeated addition of a number is equivalent to multiplying by that number.

For example, if I add 2 to itself 3 times (2 + 2 + 2), that is equivalent to multiplying 2 times 3. In the table in problem 4, we add 3 to get from one output to the next. Therefore it might make sense to try multiplying the input values by 3. If we multiply the first input value, 2, by 3, the result is 6. Yet the output is 7. When the second input value, 3, is multiplied by 3, the result is 9. Yet the output is 10. Likewise, 4 times 3 is 12, and the output is 13. It appears as though the result when multiplying by 3 is always 1 short of the output; the rule, then, must be multiply the input by 3 and add 1. At this stage, there is no reason to use a variable in expressing the rule; however, if students are ready, they might express this rule as $y = 3x + 1$, where x is the input value and y is the output value. In later grades, students will be given relationships where repeated multiplication generates the table of inputs and outputs; these relationships are called *exponential*.

This problem can be easily combined with problem 5 to challenge students in making and interpreting a data table.

The Sticky Problem of Parallelogram Pancakes by Faye Nisonoff Ruopp and Paula Poundstone (Heinemann: Portsmouth, NH), © 2006.

5. Two Heads Are Worse Than One

This problem has a slight hitch that doesn't occur in problem 4. Notice that the input values are not in order, as they were in problem 4. This makes looking for a constant difference a bit more difficult. Students certainly can use a guess-and-check strategy to figure out the rule. However, you might encourage them to put the values in a table in order:

INPUT	OUTPUT
0	1
2	5
4	9
6	13

Ignoring the input of 0 for a moment, notice that the inputs of 2, 4, and 6 are evenly spaced, as are the outputs of 5, 9, and 13. The inputs are increasing by 2 and the outputs are increasing by 4 each time. However, if we multiply the inputs by 4, there is not a consistent rule that will yield the correct output from each input. Since the inputs are increasing by 2 each time, it might be helpful to think about the possible missing inputs (1, 3, and 5) and their respective outputs (3, 7, and 11). If for every increase of 4 in the output, there is an increase of 2 in the input, then for every increase of 2 in the output, there is an increase of 1 in the input. There is an assumption here that the relationship is linear, which students will explore in later grades. Now we can try multiplying the inputs by the difference between successive outputs (2). Testing this conjecture, and multiplying 2 by 2, we get 4, which is 1 short of the output. Likewise, multiplying 4 by 2, we get 8, again 1 short of the output. Therefore, a reasonable guess for the rule would be to double the input and add 1. This does, in fact, work for all of the inputs in the table.

One question to ask students is if the input of 0 gives them any clues as to what the rule is. In fact, for any table where the pattern has a constant increase in outputs given a constant increase in inputs, the output for an input of 0 (in this case, 1) is always the number that is added on after the multiplication. Students will learn about this characteristic in later grades.

You can combine this problem with problem 4 to challenge students in making and interpreting a data table.

6. The Greatest Rock and Roll Band That Ever Toasted a Wienie

The story setting for problem 6 relates back to problem 2 in the "Number Sense & Operations" section. In this problem, students are solving a simple equation. At this point, guessing and checking is a reasonable method. Students might reframe this problem as an addition problem: What added to 16 equals 43? Encourage them to do the calculations mentally. The answer is 27 tent poles were missing. The box in this problem is a stand-in for what will be a variable in later grades.

7. The Bushy Tale of Sour Squirrels

Problem 7 continues the story of the camping trip. In this problem there are two operations involved—multiplication and addition. Using a cover-up method is sometimes helpful in thinking about a solution. Cover "$2 \times \square$" in the equation $2 \times \square + 3 = 15$ and ask, What added to 3 equals 15? The answer would be 12. Therefore $2 \times \square$ must be 12.

The next question would be What number multiplied by 2 is 12? The answer, therefore, is that each band member gets 6 sour lemon cookies. Some students may also use a guess-and-check method here, which is certainly acceptable at this grade level. In later grades, students will develop more efficient and systematic ways of solving equations. As an extension, you can ask students to make up their own equations to solve. This enables them to think about how to construct an equation with an unknown.

Extra!, Extra!

1. Add 5 to the previous term to get any term.

2. The next figure would be four rows of four boxes in each row, and the one following would be five rows of five boxes in each row.

3. The rule is multiply the input by 5 and add 2.

4. The value of the box is 5.

Geometry

The problems that follow are in the Geometry strand. The mathematics in these problems focuses on student exploration of geometric shapes and relationships. Students in grades 4 and 5 begin to categorize shapes, identifying their properties and components, such angle measures and lengths of sides. They also look at characteristics of different shapes, such as those having line symmetry.

The topics covered in these problems were chosen from state and national standards:

- Identify and compare special types of triangles (isosceles, equilateral, right) and quadrilaterals (square, rectangle, parallelogram, rhombus, trapezoid)

- Identify angles as acute, right, or obtuse

- Identify line symmetry

The problems in this section include definitions and vocabulary. At times the definitions in geometry can be overwhelming. It may be helpful for students to keep a notebook of vocabulary terms and definitions that they can refer to. Some students also find it helpful to put these definitions on flash cards, and teachers often create word walls to display these terms.

When students are grappling with these problems, they are working with classifications of triangles and

quadrilaterals. It may be helpful to illustrate the classifications with a chart that shows the relationships, moving from the general (quadrilaterals or triangles) to the
more specific subcategories (squares or equilateral triangles). Also, students will realize that some of the classifications of triangles concentrate on the lengths of sides,
and others focus on the measures of the angles.

Big League Geometry

It's the dream of many a young person to play someday for the California Angels. However, because of a misprint on his dream form, Leonardo Digit got an opportunity to play for the California Angles, a geometry team. It's harder than it sounds. He got injured in his first game. You've got to come off the bench and replace him. Here's your first problem.

See this drawing of part of a triangle? Complete the drawing so that the triangle is equilateral. And be careful, this is exactly how Leonardo got hurt.

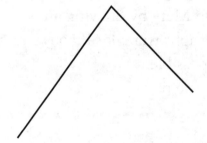

Isosceles Cheese

Mary loved to go to her room to just think about
Danny O. Cool Guy Rock Star. He was the greatest
rock star, the coolest guy, and the most, well…
Danny O., I guess. She had 23 framed color photographs of him, each with a slightly different hair-
style. She spent hours listening to his hit CD, *I Am
Danny O. Cool Guy Rock Star. Duh*. While rear-
ranging the 23 framed photographs on the wall for
maximum eye contact, she had left a lot of holes
in the wall.

She decided to paint a yellow isosceles triangle
over some of the holes in a corner to make it look
like swiss cheese. Can you help Mary by drawing an
isosceles triangle that is also a right triangle? If you
cannot, explain why it is not possible.

Quick—she already bought the paint.

The Sticky Problem of Parallelogram Pancakes by Faye Nisonoff Ruopp and Paula Poundstone (Heinemann: Portsmouth, NH), © 2006.

The Sticky Problem of Parallelogram Pancakes

Mary's mother wasn't too happy about the walls in Mary's room. Naturally, she wanted to encourage Mary to creatively express her feelings about Danny O. Cool Guy Rock Star and swiss cheese, but when it involved holes in the wall, that was a costly matter. So, when Mary asked for money to buy a concert ticket, Mary's mother dropped the hammer. Mary had to get a job.

She was in luck. The House of Parallelogram Pancakes urgently needed a new cook. It's her first night and the restaurant is packed. Mary's slightly too big uniform is covered in pancake batter. Her chef's hat is dripping with eggs and there's a line of angry waiters and waitresses waiting for Mary to cook the orders for their customers.

A tall waitress with a trapezoid-shaped bun on her head (the shape of the food pyramid with no point, which reminds Mary that she hasn't eaten enough grains today) yells, "I need a parallelogram-shaped pancake that is not a rhombus."

Can you draw the pancake for her?

The Sticky Problem of Parallelogram Pancakes by Faye Nisonoff Ruopp and Paula Poundstone (Heinemann: Portsmouth, NH), © 2006.

Rhombus Rules

The parallelogram pancakes that aren't rhombuses are going like hotcakes. Mary is thinking she has kind of got the hang of this. Her feet are glued to the floor with pancake batter, but she feels good. Or she did, but now a short, red-faced waitress has appeared before her, banging on the stainless steel slide and yelling, "I need a large stack of rhombus-shaped pancakes that are not parallelograms!"

Mary is in a panic. She doesn't know if such a shape can be made, let alone in pancakes. Danny O. Cool Guy Rock Star hasn't done any songs about that. How could she possibly know? Can you draw a rhombus that is not a parallelogram for her? Explain why or why not.

The Sticky Problem of Parallelogram Pancakes by Faye Nisonoff Ruopp and Paula Poundstone (Heinemann: Portsmouth, NH), © 2006.

Plenty of Rectangle Pancakes for Miranda Morandmore

Half of the House of Parallelogram Pancakes has been taken over by the birthday party for five-year-old Miranda Morandmore. Poor Mary has been slammed with an order for twenty rectangle pancakes that aren't squares. It's an emergency. These five-year-olds are wild and the clown with the balloon animals isn't very good. He can only make snakes. The birthday kiddies are sucking down syrup right out of the container and bodysurfing across the floor on the butter patties. The parents are stuck to the ceiling and the waitresses are hiding behind the "Please Wait to Be Seated" sign. The little birthday princess and her pals are headed for the whipped cream. Please draw a rectangle that is not a square so Mary can copy it. She's drawing a blank.

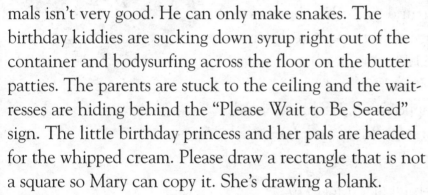

The Sticky Problem of Parallelogram Pancakes by Faye Nisonoff Ruopp and Paula Poundstone (Heinemann: Portsmouth, NH), © 2006.

Can't Hold Back the Hits of Danny O. Cool Guy Rock Star

Tonight is the night. Danny O. Cool Guy Rock Star is in concert. The hall is packed. There hasn't been this kind of excitement in this town since the California Angles played the Oklahoma Protractors. There is electricity in the air and a little bit of pancake batter in Mary's hair. She's right smack in the front row, ready to rock.

Danny O. Cool Guy Rock Star is getting ready to jump on stage with a split leap and wail when he peeks through the curtain at the stage and starts to freak out.

"Oh, no. Look, man, I need a rectangle-shaped stage that is not a parallelogram or I can't go on."

Oh, this is going to be disappointing. He has a brand-new song about his number-one fan Mary, too. It's called "My Little Pancake Flipper," and it goes like this:

Watching you flip pancakes is all that it takes to
make my heart go boom, boom, boom
My heartstrings play like a fiddle
as I watch you work that griddle.
But I can't think of anything to rhyme with
spatula, not to mention parallelogram.

The Sticky Problem of Parallelogram Pancakes by Faye Nisonoff Ruopp and Paula Poundstone (Heinemann: Portsmouth, NH), © 2006.

It can be sung to the tune of any song. The lyrics are so brilliant, Danny O. didn't worry too much about the notes.

Can you please draw a rectangle that is not a parallelogram so his stage crew can build it? Explain why or why not. It's unfair to keep this soul-stirring music from the fans a minute longer.

The Sticky Problem of Parallelogram Pancakes by Faye Nisonoff Ruopp and Paula Poundstone (Heinemann: Portsmouth, NH), © 2006.

The Troubling Case of the Missing Trapezoid Parts

I'm sorry to say it, but here's all that's left of your trapezoid. I don't know what could have happened to it. There was a gang of erasers in the alley last night that looked like they were up to no good, but there's also been an epidemic of White-Out spills in the area. It's tough to say without an investigation. Don't panic. Calmly complete the drawing of this trapezoid so we can help solve the case.

The Sticky Problem of Parallelogram Pancakes by Faye Nisonoff Ruopp and Paula Poundstone (Heinemann: Portsmouth, NH), © 2006.

8

Covering All of the Angles with the Polygon Police

Having drawn a picture of your missing trapezoid in problem 7, you call the polygon police. You study your trapezoid so you can report the incident.

A. Grand Theft Trapezoid

"Polygon Police, Sergeant Point speaking," says a gruff voice when you call. You explain that sometime last night part of your trapezoid went missing. "Remain calm," he says.

"I feel calm. It's just a trapezoid. It's not that big a deal," you answer.

"You may be in shock."

"Gee, I don't think so. I'm just calling because I'm supposed to for this problem in the workbook."

"I see. Well, could you describe your trapezoid? How many right angles does it have?"

Tell him how many right angles your trapezoid has.

B. **All-Points Bulletin for a Cute Little Trapezoid**

"Thank you. I see," Sergeant Point continues. "Could you tell me how many acute angles your trapezoid has?"

"None of the angles are really cute," you answer.

"Are you on a cell phone? Acute, not cute, *acute* angles. Could you tell me how many acute angles your trapezoid has, and could you estimate their measure? And could you hurry it up—I've got tickets to see the California Angles play tonight."

Tell him how many acute angles your trapezoid has, and estimate their measure.

C. **Obtuse Angles on the Loose**

"Indeedy-do," he says. "Could you tell me how many obtuse angles your trapezoid has and estimate their measure?"

"I don't think I'm supposed to talk about obtuse angles or their measure over the phone to a stranger," you answer.

"Just write it down then."

You write it down.

The Sticky Problem of Parallelogram Pancakes by Faye Nisonoff Ruopp and Paula Poundstone (Heinemann: Portsmouth, NH), © 2006.

D. Straight Talk About the Trapezoid from Sergeant Ray Point

"Draw any lines of symmetry in your trapezoid as well, while you're at it," says Sergeant Ray Point. Do what he says. But you're probably beginning to wonder why Sergeant Ray Point doesn't know the answers to some of his own questions.

"Anything else you can tell me about your trapezoid, kid?" the sergeant asks. "Look, kid, there are lots of polygons out there. You'd be surprised how many people call to report a missing trapezoid and it turns out it wasn't even a closed figure, let alone a trapezoid. A trapezoid looks sort of like a food pyramid without the sweets and fats. By the way, do you know anybody who's not chained to the kitchen table who could eat six to eleven servings of cereal or grains a day? Chickens don't eat six to eleven servings of grain a day. Who came up with the numbers in the food pyramid? The guy from the oatmeal box?"

"Uh, yeah, um, good point, Sergeant. Look, I gotta go!"

You hang up the phone and head to the kitchen to get started on your grains. Don't forget about those lines of symmetry.

The Pentagon: Number One on Every Kid's Wish List

Lately now, Alley and Thomas E do not share well at all. Anything that Thomas E gets, Alley insists she must have the exact same thing, and anything that Alley has, Thomas E wails that he must have its twin. They each have one chopstick. It can take days for them to eat Chinese-food dinners. I bought them this beautiful pentagon to celebrate Astrid Lindgren's birthday. Even on this special occasion I don't think they'll be able to share nicely. How many lines of symmetry does it have in case I have to divide it up so each half looks the same as the other? It'd be a shame though, huh?

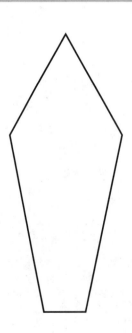

Geometry

Extra! Extra!

Here are a few extra geometry questions to help you be extra good at geometry. Geometry is important. It's a big world out there and you need to know all of the angles.

1. **Draw an isosceles triangle that is not equilateral.**

2. **Can you draw a right triangle that is equilateral?**

The Sticky Problem of Parallelogram Pancakes by Faye Nisonoff Ruopp and Paula Poundstone (Heinemann: Portsmouth, NH), © 2006.

3. Draw a rhombus that is also a rectangle. What is the name of the figure you have drawn?

4. Can you draw a trapezoid with two right angles?

5. A. Draw a trapezoid with one line of symmetry.

  B. How many acute angles does your trapezoid have?

  C. How many obtuse angles does your trapezoid have?

The Sticky Problem of Parallelogram Pancakes by Faye Nisonoff Ruopp and Paula Poundstone (Heinemann: Portsmouth, NH), © 2006.

Teacher Notes

1. Big League Geometry

Problem 1 requires that students know the definition of an equilateral triangle, which is a triangle with three sides of equal length. To complete the drawing, they will need to use a ruler to measure the longer side in the drawing and then make sure the third side is the same length as the other two. Students may also choose to lengthen both of the existing sides to form a larger equilateral triangle. In fact, there are an infinite number of equilateral triangles that can be completed! It is also true that if a triangle is equilateral, it is equiangular. That is, the triangle has three equal angles, each measuring 60 degrees. The study of geometry includes a great deal of vocabulary, and the more practice students have in working with these terms (in context) the better.

2. Isosceles Cheese

In problem 2, students are asked to think about two different classifications of triangles: isosceles triangles (or triangles with two sides of equal length) and right triangles (triangles that contain one right angle, that is, an angle with 90 degrees). Encourage students to try to draw several of each type and, as they do, focus on the drawings of right triangles to discover if there is a way to make two of the sides equal. In fact, the only way to make a right triangle isosceles is to construct the legs (the sides that form the right angle, not the side opposite the right angle) to

be equal. One example of such a triangle looks like this:

As an extension to this problem, ask students if they could draw an equilateral right triangle (a triangle with one right angle and all of the sides equal) or a scalene right triangle (a triangle with one right angle and no sides equal).

3. The Sticky Problem of Parallelogram Pancakes

The story in problem 3 continues the story of Mary begun in problem 2. Here, students need to know the definitions of a parallelogram (a quadrilateral, or four-sided figure, with both pairs of opposite sides parallel) and a rhombus (a parallelogram with all sides equal). Students are challenged to construct a parallelogram that does not have all of its sides equal. Here is one example:

Problem 4 presents students with the opposite challenge—a rhombus that is not a parallelogram. So problems 3 and 4 can easily be combined to emphasize these two definitions.

4. Rhombus Rules

Like problem 3, this problem continues the story of Mary begun in problem 2. In problem 4, students are asked to draw a rhombus that is not a parallelogram. The definition of a rhombus is a parallelogram with four equal sides. Therefore the waitress has asked for a pancake that is impossible to make. A follow-up question might be, Is every parallelogram a rhombus? This relates to the challenge presented in problem 3, so these two problems can easily be combined.

5. Plenty of Rectangle Pancakes for Miranda Morandmore

The story of Mary and the House of Parallelogram Pancakes continues in problem 5. In this problem, students are asked to draw a rectangle (a quadrilateral with all right angles) that is not a square (a rectangle with all sides equal). Here's one example:

6. Can't Hold Back the Hits of Danny O. Cool Guy Rock Star

In problem 6, students need to draw a rectangle that is not a parallelogram. Encourage students to try to draw such a figure; they will soon discover that it is impossible, since if there are four right angles, the opposite sides will have to be parallel.

7. The Troubling Case of the Missing Trapezoid Parts

Problem 7 introduces the term *trapezoid*. The definition of a trapezoid used in most textbooks is a quadrilateral with exactly one pair of sides parallel. Students start with this piece:

Therefore, to complete this drawing, they need to draw one of the two remaining sides parallel to one that is given, and make sure that the second drawn side is not parallel to the other given side. Two possibilities are shown here:

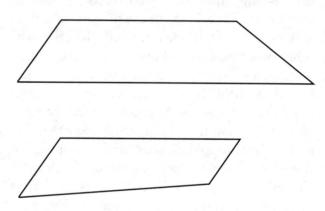

8. Covering All of the Angles with the Polygon Police

In problem 8, answers will vary according to the specific drawings that students created in problem 7. For the two drawings above, the answer to part A would be none—there are no right angles in either of these trapezoids. For part B, each trapezoid has two acute angles (angles less than 90 degrees). For part C, each trapezoid has two obtuse angles (angles greater than 90 degrees). For part D, there are no lines of symmetry for either trapezoid (lines whereby if the figure were folded in half over them, the two halves would match exactly). If students draw an isosceles trapezoid (a trapezoid with the non-parallel sides equal), there will be a line of symmetry that connects the midpoints of the parallel sides.

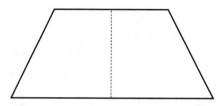

9. The Pentagon: Number One on Every Kid's Wish List

The pentagon in problem 9 has one line of symmetry, shown as follows:

In general, a line of symmetry has the following properties: If you fold the figure over the line of symmetry, the sides and vertices will match up exactly. Each point on the figure has a reflection point that is the same distance from the line of symmetry. As an extension, ask students to look around them to find objects that have lines of symmetry.

Extra! Extra!

1.

2. No. In a right triangle, the side opposite the right angle (the hypotenuse) is always larger than any of the other two sides.

3.

This is a square.

4. Yes.

5. A.

B. For the trapezoid in 5A above, there are two acute angles.

C. For the trapezoid in 5A above, there are two obtuse angles.

The Sticky Problem of Parallelogram Pancakes by Faye Nisonoff Ruopp and Paula Poundstone (Heinemann: Portsmouth, NH), © 2006.

$\mathcal{M}$easurement

$\mathcal{T}$he problems that follow are in the Measurement strand. The mathematics in these problems develops students' ability to select appropriate units of measurement for given contexts. In addition, students in grades 4 and 5 need to know how to convert from one unit to another. Students use measurement to calculate the area and perimeter of triangles and rectangles, using the appropriate units.

The topics covered in these problems were chosen from state and national standards:

• Select the appropriate type of unit for measuring length, area, weight, and volume

• Estimate and find the area and perimeter of a rectangle and a triangle by measuring or using diagrams or grids

• Determine simple unit conversions within a system of measurement (e.g., hours to minutes, cents to dollars, yards to feet, feet to inches, etc.)

My, How You've Grown

Units are important because words like *big*, *huge*, and even *enormous* are relative to whoever uses them, which I learned the hard way when I accidentally used an ant as my real estate agent. His face looked so big on the bus bench ad. How was I to know?

If you were measuring your own height, which of the following units might you use? Circle all that make sense.

A.   inches
B.   pounds
C.   miles
D.   kilometers
E.   feet

The Sticky Problem of Parallelogram Pancakes by Faye Nisonoff Ruopp and Paula Poundstone (Heinemann: Portsmouth, NH), © 2006.

2

$\mathcal{M}$ary Had a Little Room

Mary measured the area of her bedroom. Which of the following might be possible measurements for the area?

A. 120 square feet
B. 120 feet
C. 120 cubic feet
D. 120 yards
E. 120 pounds

Whatever you do, do not check the answers below.

Baby Fat

If a liter of water weighs about 1 kilogram, what might be a good estimate for the weight of an average infant?

A.   3 kg
B.   3 lbs.
C.   35 kg
D.   350 kg

Which would crush the proud mother on the first feeding?

The Sticky Problem of Parallelogram Pancakes by Faye Nisonoff Ruopp and Paula Poundstone (Heinemann: Portsmouth, NH), © 2006.

A Rectangle Without a Perimeter or an Area Doesn't Do Anybody Any Good at All

Using a ruler, find the perimeter and the area of the rectangle below.

Be sure to include the units in your answer. Oh, and also put the ruler away when you're done.

Did you put the ruler away?

A Long Line of Royal Losers

Prince Charming has become unbearable to be around. He still can't find the new love of his life, a marathon-running heartthrob. He's feeling hopeless, which is never a good thing, and his singing is now starting to bum everyone out. The royal family has begun to snap at one another a bit. While the Prince sat, wearing one boot, slowly and sadly eating his royal toast into the shape of a broken heart one morning, he moaned, "I fear I shall never find my love, Mother dear."

"I fear you're going to attract the royal rats by getting crumbs all over the floor," answered his mother. "What are you sitting here for? If you want to find something, you have to look for it. You're just like your father. He couldn't find his throne if we didn't keep it in the throne room."

"You're right, Mother dear. I shall search the world over to find the one who lights up my heart."

The Queen rolled her eyes. "Look, Son, be realistic. You're not going to 'search the world over.' Set achievable goals. Begin by dividing the map of the kingdom into triangles. Then, clean up your toast crumbs. Then search one of the triangles of the kingdom each day."

"All right, Mother dearest," he said, pouting as he drew the triangle below, "but first, where's my other boot?"

Find the area of the triangle on the grid below, the first triangle the Prince searched. Each grid mark is one unit.

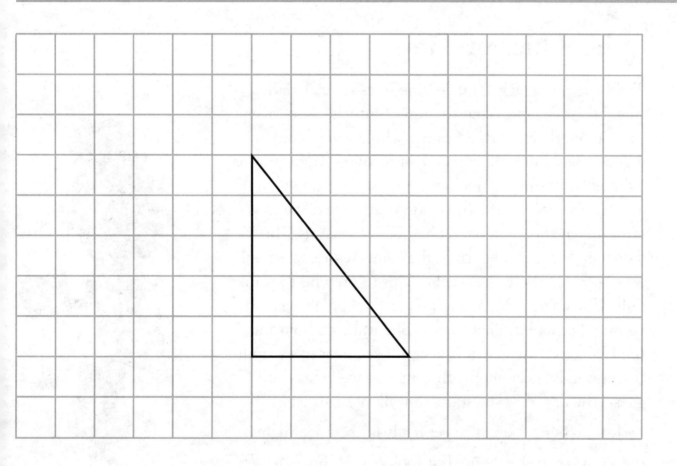

The Sticky Problem of Parallelogram Pancakes by Faye Nisonoff Ruopp and Paula Poundstone (Heinemann: Portsmouth, NH), © 2006.

The Thief of Time

Toshia is in the eighth grade. She likes to read, dance, sing, bike ride, and listen to music. But what she loves to do more than anything in the whole wide world is waste time. She could get a job at a college right now as a professor of time wasteology. She eats rice one grain at a time. She doesn't use the guide words when she looks up words in the dictionary. She doesn't even use the alphabet. She has a booth at the Time Wasters Festival every spring, where she teaches kids to pretend to drink milk. She charges $5.00 each but asks people to pay in pennies because it takes longer. She waits an hour for the bus before she gets in the car. If she ever has a traditional wedding ceremony, they may as well seat the guests the day after she starts to walk down the aisle.

It took her $5\frac{1}{4}$ hours to get ready for bed one night; then it was time to get up. If it took her $5\frac{1}{4}$ hours to get ready for bed, how many minutes was that?

The Sticky Problem of Parallelogram Pancakes by Faye Nisonoff Ruopp and Paula Poundstone (Heinemann: Portsmouth, NH), © 2006.

Mmm, You Stink Cheap

There's a cent sale at the scent store. All of the perfumes, for this week only, are available at a discount when you pay in cents. You can stink like your favorite movie star for only cents—lots and lots of cents.

On the less expensive side, for this week only, you can buy a delicate 1-gallon bottle of the very popular Attracts Bees perfume for only $6.32 in cents.

How many cents is that?

Pigs by Popular Demand

In the wake of his animals' overwhelming success in their interdenominational holiday pageant, Farmer Brown decided to create a living pig sculpture for the art lovers in their community. There was a great buzz of excitement throughout the town. Busloads of tourists lurched toward the park on the morning of the unveiling. Farmer Brown grew sideburns. He worked feverishly for days before the event, training, inspiring, and organizing his pigs. He labored without sleep for the last 24 hours before his presentation.

Finally, at the dawn's first light of morning, in front of thousands of spectators, Farmer Brown cut the line of the makeshift curtain to reveal a 423-foot-long row of pigs, standing end to end, motionless, in total silence. For a moment, no one made a sound. Then the entire crowd chorused, "Ooh!" Only one pig broke ranks and grunted. Some people still believe it was a planned part of the show, but anyone who speaks pig knows it meant "Could you get your bottom out of my face?"

The Sticky Problem of Parallelogram Pancakes by Faye Nisonoff Ruopp and Paula Poundstone (Heinemann: Portsmouth, NH), © 2006.

The effect on the crowd was deep and lasting. Some people wept. Many people were moved to ponder the meaning of life. People treated one another with more kindness afterward. Vandalism decreased. The inside of cars stayed cleaner longer after they were vacuumed.

People didn't all agree on the meaning of the living pig sculpture, but they all believed it was an important work that had changed them.

How many yards are in a 423-foot-long row of pigs?

The Sticky Problem of Parallelogram Pancakes by Faye Nisonoff Ruopp and Paula Poundstone (Heinemann: Portsmouth, NH), © 2006.

9 Measurement

Problem

The, Like, Problem with "Like"

Like, I have really been trying to, like, not say "like" when, like, it doesn't, like, help my, like, sentence say, like, what I want to, like, say. Like, language is, like, of the people, like, it changes, like, based on how people, like, use it. So, like, I can say "like," like, if I want to, but, like, it slows down, like, what I'm trying to say. So, like, I'm trying to get out of the habit. Like. It hasn't been, like, easy. If I can, like, go a whole day, like, without saying like, how many seconds would that be?

I'd, like, like it if you'd tell me.

Time Off from Time-Out

My son, Thomas E, who is in the second grade, wants to switch schools because he says there's too much time-out at his school. Time-out is when you sit on the side of the playground during recess because you insist on pushing, shoving, and grabbing from your friends in what adults call "overly aggressive play." The idea that he could avoid the dreaded time-out by simply climbing on the equipment in the yard instead of on his friend Franco's head hasn't really occurred to him. I told him that our school's time-outs are 15 minutes but the other schools in the district have 900-second time-outs. Suddenly our school looked a lot better to him. Should it? Why or why not?

The Sticky Problem of Parallelogram Pancakes by Faye Nisonoff Ruopp and Paula Poundstone (Heinemann: Portsmouth, NH), © 2006.

Measurement

Extra! Extra!

Measurement is very important. People who can't do it often tear the top off their car when they drive under a bridge. So, here are some extra problems to help you nail these skills. If you are mad about having extra measurement problems, I'm sorry, but I have one question for you: If it takes you two hours to get over being mad, how many minutes is that?

1. If you were measuring your weight, which of the following units might you use? Circle all that make sense.

    A. kilometers

    B. inches

    C. pounds

    D. milligrams

    E. kilograms

2. Beckie measured the volume of a box. Which of the following might be possible units for the volume? Circle all that make sense.

    A. square feet

    B. cubic feet

    C. inches

    D. square inches

    E. cubic inches

The Sticky Problem of Parallelogram Pancakes by Faye Nisonoff Ruopp and Paula Poundstone (Heinemann: Portsmouth, NH), © 2006.

3. Draw a rectangle on a piece of paper. Find its perimeter and its area, including units.

4. Draw a right triangle. Find its perimeter and its area, including units.

5. How many seconds are there in 5.25 minutes?

6. How many cents are there in $73.45?

7. How many inches are there in 4.5 yards?

8. How many minutes are there in 2 days?

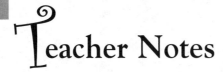

Teacher Notes

1. My, How You've Grown

Problem 1 requires that students have some understanding of the relative sizes of units of length and distance. Pounds should be eliminated first, since it is a unit of weight. Miles and kilometers are units that are too large for measuring height. Therefore, inches and feet are reasonable. Ask students to state their height in both feet and inches. As a challenge, ask students to state their height in meters (1 meter is approximately 3.28 feet).

2. Mary Had a Little Room

In problem 2, students again need to distinguish between units of area and units of length, weight, and volume. Feet and yards, pounds, and cubic feet are measures of length, weight, and volume, respectively. Therefore, the only answer that makes sense is 120 square feet. You could extend this problem by asking students, "What could be the dimensions of a room that had this area?" This kind of thinking, where students have to work backward from a solution, requires that students develop a deeper understanding of area, which they will need in later grades.

3. Baby Fat

Problem 3 states a relationship between liters, a measure of capacity, and kilograms, a measure of mass equivalent to about 2.205 pounds. Students might attempt to visualize a liter of water or milk, which is a little more than a quart. Therefore a reasonable estimate for the weight of an average infant would be 3 kilograms, or a little more than 3 quarts, or about 6.6 pounds. You may want to ask students if they know how much they weighed when they were born. Chances are the hospital used metric units to weigh them.

4. A Rectangle Without a Perimeter or an Area Doesn't Do Anybody Any Good at All

Problem 4 will have answers that vary depending upon the unit of length students use to measure the sides of the rectangle and the degree of accuracy. To find the perimeter, they should measure the sides and add them together. Since the figure is a rectangle, they can simply measure two non-parallel sides and double the sum of those two lengths. The perimeter is 15 inches. To find the area, students should multiply the lengths of two nonparallel sides. It is important that students include units in their answers. For example, if they measure the lengths in inches, the perimeter will be in inches, and the area will be in square inches. The area is 12.5 sq. in. Ask students to draw a picture of a square inch or explain what it means. As an extension, you may want to ask them to draw another rectangle with the same perimeter but a different area. In later grades, they will determine which rectangle with a given perimeter has the greatest area. Such problems fall under the category of optimization.

5. A Long Line of Royal Losers

The story in problem 5 takes us back to the story of Prince Charming that we encountered in problem 1 of the "Number Sense & Operations" chapter. In problem 5, students need to know the formula for the area of a triangle. This is not meant to be an estimation problem, in which students would count the number of squares and parts of squares covered by the triangle to come up with an estimate. Here they need to find the length of each leg of the right triangle and use the formula for the area of a triangle:

$$\frac{1}{2} \times \text{base} \times \text{height} = \text{area}$$

For this triangle, the area would be $\frac{1}{2} \times 4 \times 5$, or 10 square units.

Another strategy for finding the area, if students forget the formula, is to create a rectangle from the triangle by rotating the triangle 180° about the midpoint of the hypotenuse.

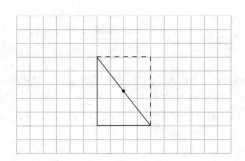

The area of this rectangle is 5 units × 4 units, or 20 square units. Therefore the area of half of the rectangle, or the area of the triangle, is 10 square units. As an extension, ask students if they can find a different right triangle with the same area.

6. The Thief of Time

Problems 6 through 10 involve converting from one unit of measure to another. Problem 6 involves measures of time, and students need to know the number of minutes in an hour (60). To find the number of minutes in $5\frac{1}{4}$ hours, we need to multiply $5\frac{1}{4}$ by 60. There are several ways to multiply by $5\frac{1}{4}$.

One way would be to multiply 60 first by 5 ($60 \times 5 = 300$) and then take one-quarter of 60, which is 15. Next add 300 to 15; the answer is that it took 315 minutes for Toshia to get to bed.

Another method would be to change $5\frac{1}{4}$ to an improper fraction, $\frac{21}{4}$, and then multiply this by 60. This would give you $\frac{1,260}{4}$, which is 315. A final method would be to change $5\frac{1}{4}$ to a decimal number, 5.25, and then multiply by 60.

Here's a possible extension question: If you live to be 90, and you sleep 8 hours a day, how many seconds of your life are you awake?

7. Mmm, You Stink Cheap

Problems 6 through 10 involve converting from one unit of measure to another. Problem 7 involves units of money, and students need to change the cost of the perfume from dollars to cents. Since there are 100 cents in a dollar, we need to multiply 6.32 by 100. Students can do this by hand, or they may recognize that when multiplying by 100, you move the decimal two places to the right. The answer is 632 cents. Another way to think about this problem is to first consider that there are 6 dollars, and in every dollar there are 100 cents. That makes 600 cents. Then we can add the additional 32 cents to get 632 cents.

An extension problem: Calculate the number of dimes needed to pay $6.32 in dimes. How many pennies would you still need?

8. Pigs by Popular Demand

Problems 6 through 10 involve converting from one unit of measure to another. Problem 8 uses measures of length, and students need to know that there are 3 feet in a yard. The next task is to decide whether to multiply 423 by 3 or divide 423 by 3. An important question to consider initially is whether the answer should be smaller or larger than 423. The number of yards should be less than the number of feet, since a yard is longer than a foot, and therefore it makes sense to divide 423 by 3. The answer is 141 yards. Students will encounter conversions throughout their mathematics careers, in both science and mathematics.

9. The Problem with "Like"

Problems 6 through 10 involve converting from one unit of measure to another. In problem 9, students need to know several time-conversion facts. Going from the smallest measure of time in the problem to the largest, there are 60 seconds in a minute, 60 minutes in an hour, and 24 hours in a day. To find the number of seconds in an hour, then, we need to multiply:

$$\frac{60 \text{ seconds}}{\text{minute}} \times \frac{60 \text{ seconds}}{\text{hour}} = \frac{3{,}600 \text{ seconds}}{\text{hour}}$$

Note that we can think about multiplying the units as well, so that minutes divided by minutes is 1, and we are left with seconds/hour.

$$\frac{\text{seconds}}{\text{minute}} \times \frac{\text{minutes}}{\text{hour}} = \frac{\text{seconds}}{\text{hour}}$$

Because there are 24 hours in a day, we can multiply again:

$$\frac{3{,}600 \text{ seconds}}{\text{hour}} \times \frac{24 \text{ hours}}{\text{day}} = \frac{86{,}400 \text{ seconds}}{\text{day}}$$

Here again we can think about the hours divided by hours as 1, leaving the units of seconds/day.

$$\frac{\text{seconds}}{\text{hour}} \times \frac{\text{hours}}{\text{day}} = \frac{\text{seconds}}{\text{day}}$$

Therefore, if the speaker in the problem went an entire day without saying "like," she would be going 86,400 seconds without saying the word.

10. Time Off from Time-Out

Problems 6 through 10 involve converting from one unit of measure to another. In problem 10, students need to compare 900 seconds with 15 minutes, which will entail a conversion. They can convert either 900 seconds to minutes or 15 minutes to seconds. Most students will prefer to convert 15 minutes to seconds, because it involves multiplication rather than division. Since there are 60 seconds in a minute,

$$15 \text{ minutes} \times \frac{60 \text{ seconds}}{\text{minute}} = 900 \text{ seconds}$$

Therefore, the length of the time-outs at all schools is the same. Thomas E's school should not look any better, but not any worse either!

Extra! Extra!

1. C. pounds or E. kilograms
2. B. cubic feet or E. cubic inches
3. Answers will vary.
4. Answers will vary.
5. 315 seconds
6. 7,345 cents
7. 162 inches
8. 2,880 minutes

The Sticky Problem of Parallelogram Pancakes by Faye Nisonoff Ruopp and Paula Poundstone (Heinemann: Portsmouth, NH), © 2006.

Data Analysis, Statistics & Probability

The problems that follow are in the Data Analysis, Statistics, and Probability strand. The mathematics in these problems focuses on developing students' data analysis skills as they look at data as a set with collective properties. Students in grades 4 and 5 learn to construct and analyze different representations of data as well as measures of central tendency. This strand also includes a beginning study of probability, as students determine outcomes and probabilities for simple events.

The topics covered in these problems were chosen from state and national standards:

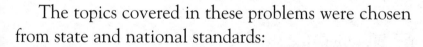

• Construct representations of data sets using tables, bar graphs, pictographs, line graphs, circle graphs, and tallies

• Determine possible outcomes for simple situations, such as drawing a particular color of marble from a bag

• Determine mean, median, mode, maximum, minimum, and range of a set of data

Data Analysis, Statistics & Probability

Once Upon a Mud Pie

After breaking things off with Prince Charming, Cinderella became a lacrosse coach. She had great success coaching in a town on Long Island, New York. The sport really grew in popularity after her arrival. She decided to record the number of children who were playing lacrosse in leagues or schools there and organize the information so she could plan for next year's lacrosse program. She was sitting with a folder full of graphs and data on the bleachers by the field, watching a team practice, when a brisk fall wind came up and scattered her papers hither and yon. When she leaped up to grab them, her glass slipper caught on a bleacher, and she fell through the bottom into the mud below. Her ball gown went up over her head, and by the time she wrestled it back down, both she and the gown were smudged, splotched, soaked, and speckled with mud. Cinderella burst into tears.

"Cinderella?" she heard a voice call.

"What?" sniffed Cinderella, looking up to find her fairy godmother in a sweat suit and cleated athletic shoes.

"What are you doing, my dear?" the fairy godmother asked.

"Oh, Fairy Godmother, I am so happy to see you. I've fallen and my papers have scattered hither and yon and I can no longer analyze my data!"

"Yeah, but what are you doing?"

"What do you mean?"

"I mean, what are you doing?"

  The Sticky Problem of Parallelogram Pancakes by Faye Nisonoff Ruopp and Paula Poundstone (Heinemann: Portsmouth, NH), © 2006.

"Right now?"

"Right now."

"Oh, well, I'm sitting…"

"In the mud."

"Yes, in the mud… and…"

"Crying."

"Yes, crying," said Cinderella, sheepishly wiping away a tear.

"Are you helping yourself, Cinderella?"

"No, not exactly."

"No, you're not. Isn't this just the kind of behavior that almost got you stuck with that singing prince? Now get up and go over yon and pick up your papers. If you need help, ask for it, but don't just sit around crying."

Cinderella collected her papers that were yon, but the hither ones she found smushed beneath her in the mud.

"I do need help, Fairy Godmother."

"That's better, my dear."

"While I go change my clothes, could you create a bar graph showing these data, create a line graph showing these data, find the range of numbers of children, find what is the maximum number of children playing lacrosse at the ages given, and find what is the minimum number of children playing lacrosse at the ages given?"

"No problem, Cin," said the fairy godmother. "I'll get you some help."

Guess who she's asking for help?

Graph like you've never graphed before! Here are the data:

AGE	CHILDREN
5	104
7	235
9	246
11	197
13	112
15	85
17	79

A. Create a bar graph showing these data.

The Sticky Problem of Parallelogram Pancakes by Faye Nisonoff Ruopp and Paula Poundstone (Heinemann: Portsmouth, NH), © 2006.

B. Create a line graph showing these data.

C. What is the range of numbers of children?

D. What is the maximum number of children playing lacrosse at the ages given?

E. What is the minimum number of children playing lacrosse at the ages given?

The Sticky Problem of Parallelogram Pancakes by Faye Nisonoff Ruopp and Paula Poundstone (Heinemann: Portsmouth, NH), © 2006.

Further Proof That Poster Board Is the Key to Higher Education

This year, Ms. Nisonoff's fifth-grade class project night, which they named Everything I Know About That, was easily the best ever. Alley sparkled with pride over a truly fantastic array of posters, pictures, and facts about diamonds. She even had a glass display case with an alarm and a black velvet stand inside with a real diamond, which disappeared about halfway through the night! Albert wore a trench coat, pipe, and hat and was equipped with intriguing information about some of the world's most confounding unsolved crimes. He even took fingerprints of the visitors to his display. The visual aid for Frankie's great white shark display had to be released back into the ocean by a marine rescue team, but it created a fabulous learning opportunity. Albert, who suspected Frankie's visual aid of the diamond theft, very much regretted not having gotten its fingerprints. Sam's display included a trunk and some handcuffs. He did a great job displaying interesting facts about the famous magician and escape artist, Harry Houdini. No one could find Sam or his bunny anywhere.

Mary had done some truly fascinating, beyond-fifth-grade-level research on phobias, but she was afraid to talk to anyone about it and mostly hid behind her posters, clutching a box of bandages that she carried just in case. Doug's amazing presentation on the history of plumbing accidentally flooded the auditorium about halfway through the night, but it made very clear the importance of Julie's project on the many uses of the sponge. Charlie's presentation, "Fruit Flies as Pets: Why It Has Never Really Taken Off," was a surprise hit. Marcus answered lots of questions for people on his fascinating topic of sports injuries. He even hit himself in the head with a lacrosse stick and thought he was a little girl named Katie for a while, which everyone agreed showed a lot of effort. Gilda researched the rules of proper and valid scientific social study and had conducted her own ministudies in the areas of hope and kindness and presented the data. She asked ten of her friends to do something helpful for someone else every day for two weeks and ten more of her friends, not to be mean of course, but to in no way go out of their way for anyone else. Then she interviewed all twenty friends about how they felt about themselves and the world. The results were dramatic and funny and moving. Gilda stood tall while she shared her research. She was busy answering questions all

night, except when she took a break to help sponge up the flood. It was a wonderful night. Albert found the diamond in the trunk of Sam's Houdini display. The bunny had taken it. What a wonderful night. Ms. Nisonoff couldn't have been more proud.

The students in Ms. Nisonoff's class kept track of how long they worked on their research projects. Here are the data from the class:

STUDENT	TIME IN MINUTES
Marcus	46
Charlie	50
Faye	24
Paula	23
Gilda	54
Allison	33
Sam	48
Elaine	27
Albert	31
Mary	32
Frankie	55
Beckie	51
Doug	18
Julie	48

A. Make a histogram of the results. Make the width of your bars in intervals of minutes.

B. What was the median time to work on the project?

C. What was the mean time to work on the project?

D. What was the mode time to work on the project?

E. Do you think Doug was really thorough?

F. Who do you think spent the most time pretending to sharpen his or her pencil?

Polling Farmer Brown

Farmer Brown is exhausted. After providing cultural events for his community while enduring the rigors of farming for the last couple of years, he's drained of energy. He feels like an empty balloon that just flew backward across the room, sputtering out its spitty air. In order to focus his energies most effectively next year, he took a poll to determine which of his projects his patrons liked best.

20% liked his cow talent contest (Bovine Idol)

25% liked his interdenominational holiday pageant

10% liked swimming with his chickens

40% liked his living pig sculpture

5% liked his brussels sprouts

Please draw a circle graph of their preferences.

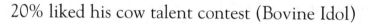

The Sticky Problem of Parallelogram Pancakes by Faye Nisonoff Ruopp and Paula Poundstone (Heinemann: Portsmouth, NH), © 2006.

The Probability of Charlie Losing His Marbles

Charlie thought he lost his marbles, but he really didn't. He found a bag of them behind Marcus' enormous collection of lacrosse balls. Someone had been messing with them, though. There used to be 5 red marbles, 6 green marbles, and 4 yellow marbles. Someone, for some unknown reason, took out the green marbles and put in 6 moldy grapes and took out the red marbles and put in 5 *eyeballs!* The eyeballs might have been fake. Charlie didn't know. He was so grossed out when he glanced in the bag that he closed it quickly so he wouldn't throw up in it and make his situation much worse. It made no sense. Charlie was the nicest guy in the world. He didn't even kill mosquitoes; he used positive encouragement to

The Sticky Problem of Parallelogram Pancakes by Faye Nisonoff Ruopp and Paula Poundstone (Heinemann: Portsmouth, NH), © 2006.

get them not to bite. Why would anyone be so cruel as to put disgusting stuff in his marble bag?

That's not actually the question. Here is the question: If Charlie closes his eyes, reaches into the bag without gagging, and pulls out one item, what is the probability that it will be an *eyeball?*

If Charlie puts the item back and reaches in again—is he crazy? There's disgusting stuff in there! Ew. That's not the question, though. Here's the question:

What is the probability that the next item he pulls out will *not* be a yellow marble?

The Sticky Problem of Parallelogram Pancakes by Faye Nisonoff Ruopp and Paula Poundstone (Heinemann: Portsmouth, NH), © 2006.

Extra! Extra!

The only way to get good at something is to practice. Think of something you do every day. I'll bet you're good at it. Like breathing, for example. You breathe every day, right? And I'll bet you're good at it. So, here's your chance to get just as good at data analysis, statistics, and probability.

1. Create a bar graph to show the populations of the five cities listed below:

Farmington	10,000
Bayside	4,500
Jamesburg	8,000
Newton	80,000
Yorkville	15,000

2. The Yale Lacrosse Team posted the number of goals each of its players scored one season. Coach Shay was quite proud. The results were as follows:

1, 1, 1, 1, 1, 2, 2, 2, 3, 4, 4, 4, 5, 5, 7, 9, 9, 11, 11, 15, 18

A. Make a histogram of the results.

B. Find the median number of goals scored.

The Sticky Problem of Parallelogram Pancakes by Faye Nisonoff Ruopp and Paula Poundstone (Heinemann: Portsmouth, NH), © 2006.

C. Find the mean number of goals scored.

D. Find the range for the number of goals scored.

$3.$ Look at the following circle graph.

If the sector labeled "apples" represents 40% of the collection, what must the measure of the central angle be for that sector?

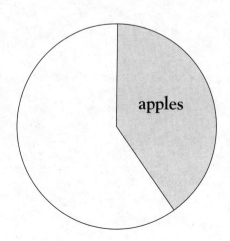

4. If you choose a marble from a bag that has 6 yellow marbles and 9 red marbles, what is the probability that the marble will be yellow? Not yellow?

5. If you toss one die, what is the probability the number that lands will be even?

1. Once Upon a Mud Pie

In part A of problem 1, students need to know how to create a bar graph from a table of data. In a bar graph, either horizontal or vertical bars are used to display the data. If we use vertical bars here, the first thing we need to do is to choose a vertical scale. Since the numbers of children range from 79 to 246, increments of 10 or 20 might be reasonable. On the horizontal axis, the bars would be labeled with the ages of the children. A possible graph might be:

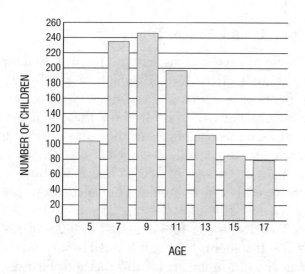

In part B, the data in the table needs to be displayed in a line graph, a graph where points are plotted to represent each data point (age, children). The scale for the vertical axis can be similar to the one created in part A, and increments of 1 for the horizontal axis are reasonable. A possible graph might be:

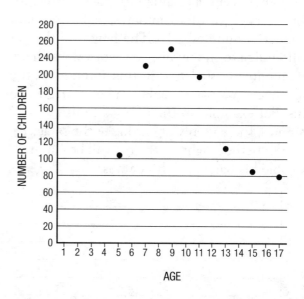

Although the problem asks for a "line" graph, the points on the graph should *not* be connected since we cannot be certain about the number of children in years between the ages given. A continuous line implies information about all points along the horizontal axis.

Part C asks for the range of numbers, or the difference between the greatest and least values. The range of numbers of children, then, would be 246 − 79, or 167.

In part D, students need to find the maximum, or greatest, number of children playing lacrosse, which is 246. The answer to part E is 79. As an extension, you may want to ask students which graph gives them the most information about the number of children playing lacrosse.

2. Further Proof That Poster Board Is the Key to Higher Education

In problem 2, part A, students are asked to make a histogram, a graph that displays the frequency of data. The first step in creating a histogram is to create equal intervals for the horizontal axis, which will be the width of the bars. Intervals of 5 minutes seem appropriate. It may be reasonable to begin with 15 minutes, since the least number of minutes is 18. The height of the bar will designate the number of data values (here, the number of students) in that interval, or the frequency. A separate table can be created to do this. For example, in the interval from 15 to 20 minutes, there is only one value in the table, 18. Therefore the height for the bar will be 1 unit. A possible histogram for this data is

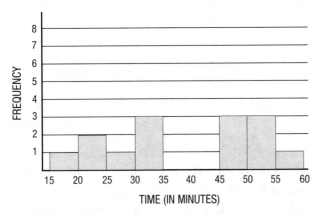

To find the median time in part B, we need to put the values of minutes in order, from least to greatest. The median is the middle number. If there are an even number of values, the median is the average of the two middle numbers. In this case, the values arranged in order are 18, 23, 24, 27, 31, 32, 33, 46, 48, 48, 50, 51, 54, 55. The middle two values are 33 and 46; therefore the median is the average of 33 and 46:

$$\frac{(33 + 46)}{2} = 39.5.$$

To find the mean time in part C, students need to find the sum of all of the times and then divide by the number of data values (in this case, 14). The sum of the values is 540, and therefore the mean is $\frac{540}{14}$ or 38.57. Another way to visualize the mean is to consider equalizing the amounts. Imagine these times as stacks of chips, side by side. For example, 18 minutes would be represented by a stack of 18 chips. Now consider taking these 14 stacks and trying to make them all the same height by moving or adding chips to each stack. To make the stacks even, we would have about 38.57 chips per stack, assuming we could cut these chips into decimal pieces! To extend this problem, ask students if there is a way to add two additional times and not change either the median or the mean.

The mode time in part D is the time that occurs most often. In the table, the value of 48 occurs twice and is therefore the mode.

3. Polling Farmer Brown

Problem 3 requires students to use a protractor to draw a circle (or pie) graph, a graph that reflects the percentages given as sectors. Students need to consider how these percentages relate to the angles of the sectors. Since a circle has 360 degrees, we need to take the individual percentages of 360 to figure out how to create each central angle. The calculations are as follows: 20% of 360 = 72; 25% of 360 = 90; 10% of 360 = 36; 40% of 360 = 144; 5% of 360 = 18. If students have not learned how to take a percent of a number, try this method: First ask them to figure out what 10% of 360 is by thinking about a number that you could add 10 times to get 360. Once they have 10% (or 36), they can easily find 20% and 40%. If they know 10%, they also know 5% (half of 10%), and that allows them to find 25%. Students can then use a protractor to construct the angles representing each of the percentages. Here's how the circle graph should look:

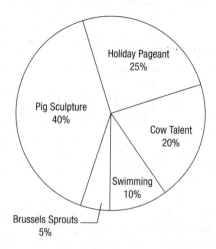

4. The Probability of Charlie Losing His Marbles

Charlie's bag includes 15 items:

4 yellow marbles

6 moldy grapes

5 eyeballs

In the first part of problem 4, since only 5 objects are eyeballs, the probability of Charlie pulling an eyeball out is $\frac{5}{15}$ or $\frac{1}{3}$. In general, to calculate the probability of an event, we need to find the number of ways that event occurs (in this case, 5) and divide it by the total number of outcomes (in this case, 15). As an extension, ask, "If you know the probability of an event, how can you find the probability that the event will not occur?"

In the second part, to find the probability that the next object Charlie pulled out would not be a yellow marble, again we can use the concept that the probability of an event (in this case, pulling an object that is not a yellow marble) is the number of ways that event occurs (in this case, there are 11 objects that are not yellow marbles) divided by the total number of outcomes (in this case, 15), which gives us $\frac{11}{15}$. In later grades, students will be asked to find the probability of pulling two marbles at the same time, or one marble and then another, with and without replacement.

Extra! Extra!

1.

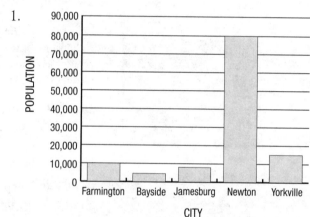

2. A.

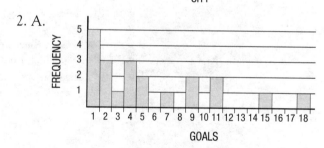

   B. 4 goals

   C. 5.52 goals

   D. 17 goals

3. 144 degrees

4. $\frac{6}{15}$, $\frac{9}{15}$

5. $\frac{3}{6}$ or $\frac{1}{2}$

The Sticky Problem of Parallelogram Pancakes by Faye Nisonoff Ruopp and Paula Poundstone (Heinemann; Portsmouth, NH), © 2006.